BLUEPRINT FOR REHABILITATION

A Positive Approach to Guidelines

City of Dayton
Department of Planning

Second Edition
May 1990

CONTENTS

INTRODUCTION

When the Oregon Historic Dictrict was first designated in 1972, there was not much interest in historic preservation in Dayton. Since then, six more districts have been locally designated (in addition to their being listed on the National Register of Historic Places) and interest in preservation is very high. Indeed, historic designation and participation in preservation has helped to spawn the revitalization of Dayton's older urban neighborhoods.

Historic district zoning enables the City of Dayton to preserve and protect its significant architectural resources without compromising the rights of private property owners to use and enjoy those resources. To ensure the success of historic district zoning, the City created the Historic Architecture Committee, now the Landmarks Commission, and charged it with the responsibility of maintaining architectural controls in locally designated historic districts and of landmark structures. These controls encourage compatible, sensitive modifications which will enhance the unique character of historic districts, thereby visibly promoting the interest of the City of Dayton in its heritage and reflecting the City's concern for the general welfare of its citizens.

The Landmarks Commission established the following guidelines to be used when making alterations to historic properties. This manual reflects more than fifteen years of Commission decisions and recommendations which have been successfully used in rehabilitation. Prescribed methods are logical and reasonable; they are designed to preserve existing fabric, not to create examples of museum quality restorations.

The primary focus of the Blueprint for Rehabilitation is on residential architecture since that category encompasses the greatest percentage of historic structures and since many elements found in other types of buildings are adaptations from residential architecture. Those elements which are unique to commercial, institutional, or industrial building have been evaluated individually. Also included is information about landscaping and neighborhood amenities since they are important streetscape elements.

Because a building's style influences the material and techniques to be used in its maintenance or rehabilitation, identification of a building's style elements is the first step in a rehabilitation process. Thus, the manual presents local examples of nineteenth and twentieth century architectural styles and provides general characteristics of each style as well as a specific description and history of each example.

Information about individual building elements is presented with those elements being classified by function— Structural, Style, and Supplemental. Structural elements are mandatory for the continued existence and function of the building. Style elements give a building its identity and classify its construction period. Supplemental elements are functional in nature but must be decorative as well so as not to detract from the building's style; these elements should be secondary to the dominant theme of the building.

The *New Construction* section addresses proportion, scale, rhythm, and massing within a building and its relationship to other buildings on the street. This relationship is important because buildings in an urban setting are rarely isolated from one another. Each derives its significance, in part, from its position with respect to the others along the street, and these interrelationships among buildings carry over into considerations of landscaping and streetscape amenities.

Historic district zoning is a benefit to commercial districts as well. The surrounding residential areas often experience revival before the commercial districts. As neighborhoods become stabilized, the property owners reinvest in the neighborhoods and the surrounding commercial districts. This stabilizes or increases the amount of money that is available for spending in the neighborhood as older residents stop leaving and newer residents arrrive to rehabilitate and inhabit historic properties. Thus, there is also a section which discusses non-residential/commercial buildings. Because of changes in a building's use and function throughout the years, numerous non-residential buildings have undergone dramatic alterations. Rehabilitation of these structures requires serious consideration of the original design and an appreciation of the buildings' "front door" placement to the historic districts since they are normally situated along major thoroughfares. Consequently, their rehabilitation impacts not only the buildings and districts themselves but the City as well. The guidelines manual addresses these considerations and concludes with an extensive glossary of architectural and building terminology and a basic bibliography of sources.

This handbook offers guildelines for sensible and appropriate rehabilitation techniques for residential and non-residential buildings. It is hoped that these guidelines will assist not only in the continued revitalization of historic neighborhoods and buildings within the City but will serve as a resource for the City's other older neighborhoods and commercial buildings as well.

Blueprint for Rehabilitation accompanies the Revised Historic District Ordinance sections of the Dayton Revised Code of General Ordinances. This publication does not substitute for the Ordinance nor does it eliminate the requirements specified in the Ordinance. The Landmarks Commission must review and approve all work to the exterior of a property in a historic district or on the landmarks list prior to the initiation of that work.

ARCHITECTURAL STYLES

FEDERAL

RUBICON FARM
1815 BROWN STREET

Built 1816
Patterson Homestead

Many of the elements of the Federal style were borrowed from designs popular in England. Symmetry, delicate ornamentation and the use of geometric forms were elements common to architecture in both England and the U.S.

As the style made its way into the Midwest, it was greatly simplified. Smooth, symmetrical facades with long multi-paned windows were framed by end wall chimneys. Buildings were rectangular in shape, on low foundations and a long side of the rectangle served as the streetface. Ornamentation was minimal and was usually limited to the door surround.

Rubicon Farm is a two-story brick structure with a low pitched gable roof, grouped chimneys and a two-story southeast corner porch. It features a symmetrical plan with long rectangular windows and a small entry portico on the north side. Surrounding the entry doors are multi-paned glass sidelights and transoms.

The Farm was built by frontiersman Robert Patterson. His famous grandson, John Henry Patterson, founder of the National Cash Register Company, was raised at the Homestead. The latter's son Frederick donated the property to Montgomery County as an educational facility and museum.

CLASSICAL REVIVAL

OLD COURTHOUSE
7 NORTH MAIN STREET

Built 1850
Montgomery County Historical Society

The Classical Revival style, popular between 1820 and 1860, includes the Greek and Roman Revival styles. Both emulated the forms common centuries earlier to their namesakes in Europe. Greek Revival was by far the more popular of the two styles.

Pure Greek Revival featured a pedimented roof with a wide cornice supported by colossal columns, presenting the impression of a Greek temple. Simpler versions did not use the temple, but by placing columns flat against the wall face (called pilasters), provided a similar impression. Sometimes the pediment, or triangle, was broken. It did not form a complete triangle; the horizontal line only would begin its return from the diagonals.

Roman Revival employed the temple form also, but its highlights were a raised first story and a window set in the pediment. Many times, Roman Revival buildings featured hipped roofs, whereas the Greek mode used a gabled roof.

Both forms of the Classical Revival were quite symmetrical and featured very little trim. In this way the design, symbol of all that was noble and pure, appealed to all classes of people. The wealthy executed majestic temples while the workingman imitated the form and symmetry, perhaps incorporating only wide cornice and columns on a small entry porch.

The Old Courthouse is probably one of the finest examples of Greek Revival architecture in the country. It is rectangular in shape, constructed of limestone with a pediment supported by colossal columns. It has pilasters—pillars set against a wall—running the length of the building. Long windows sit between each pilaster. The rear facade has semicircular inward curving walls with a column set on each corner. The building is enhanced by a stone wall at its streetfaces.

GOTHIC REVIVAL

ALTA NURSING HOME
20 LIVINGSTON AVENUE

Built c. 1860

Romanticism flourished in mid-nineteenth century America as the nation emerged from its infancy into precocious childhood. Fantasies of knights and castles were reflected in architectural designs as well as being popular novel material.

From 1840-1860, the Gothic Revival style developed from buildings with steep gables, dormers and arched windows to intricate testimonials to the carpenter's craft. All forms of "gingerbread"—frivolous, solely decorative, details—abounded. Wall surfaces featured variety as well; many a Gothic Revival's walls featured the board and

batten technique—uniformly sized, vertical pieces of wood with narrow vertical strips used to cover seams.

Stripped of its gingerbread, the Alta Nursing Home would be a nondescript structure. Construction involved very regular application of limestone and brick for its foundation, walls and chimneys, slate for its roof, and wood for its doors and windows. Its true significance is, quite obviously, its magnificent two-story steeply gabled porch, flanking dormers, and decorative vergeboard. Small finials and pendants at the gable peaks complete the design.

ITALIAN VILLA

FIRE STATION NO. 16
31 SOUTH JERSEY STREET

Built 1909

A commanding tower is the Italian Villa style's most notable feature. It rises above the primary roofline of the building and usually features a pyramid shaped roof. The structure adjoining this square tower may be either symmetrical or asymmetrical in design. Other features of this style include straight or round-headed windows in pairs or threes, bay windows and small balconies.

Italianate style details of a low hipped roof, wide bracketed eaves and ornate window and door trim are common to the Italian Villa style, also. Both styles shared popularity during the mid-nineteenth century, though the Italian Villa

was much less prevalent. Fire Station #16, though constructed nearly thirty years after the heyday of the Italian Villa, is quite representative of the style. It features a square, pyramid roofed tower with wide eaves and brackets. The symmetrical structure has pairs of straight and round-headed windows with limestone trim. Vehicular entries with rectangular transoms are on the front (east) and north walls. Flanking the front wall rectangular entry are vehicular entries with Tudor arches. A symmetrical wing, featuring a polygonal bay and recessed second story porch, provides entry to the upper story rooms and lookout tower. The decorative dormer contributes an almost Moorish flavor.

ITALIANATE

CHARLES HUFFMAN HOUSE
49 LINDEN AVENUE

Built 1869
Harris Funeral Home

Characteristic of the Italianate style are a wide, heavily bracketed cornice and eaves over a nearly square structure. Many Italianate houses feature a flat hipped roof topped by a belvedere—or lookout tower. Simpler versions retain the cornice detail and arched windows with hood molds on the prominent facade only.

The Italianate style had its heyday between 1840 and 1880 and was used extensively in the Midwest for both residential and commercial architecture. It reflected the rising middle class who could not afford palatial mansions but exhibited their new found wealth in smaller scale with ornate detailing applied to simple structures.

The Charles Huffman House was one of the first residences to be constructed along Linden Avenue during the post Civil War building boom. It features its original belvedere, chimneys, cornice detailing, and window and door trim. Also, it boasts an unusual 1911 full length front porch with wrought iron railing and entry door with beveled glass sidelights. Completing the scene is the 1869 carriage house at the rear of the property.

OCTAGON

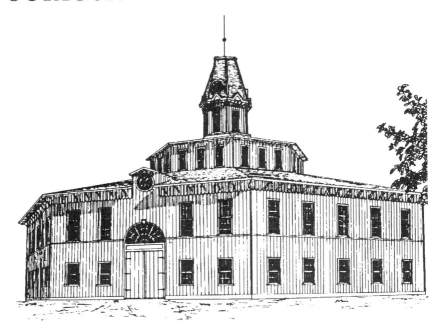

EXHIBITION BUILDING
MONTGOMERY COUNTY FAIRGROUNDS

Built 1874

Though it enjoyed only shortlived popularity (1850-1860), the innovative Octagon style was used for houses and barns throughout the nation. Eight sides, each with windows, provided excellent cross-ventilation. Building scale was maintained either by the reduction in size of upper stories or by the appearance of a size change through the use of a verandah on the lower story only. The Octagon style usually included a cupola or belvedere which rose over the building's central hall and again, provided for ventilation. Interior spaces remained rectangular with resulting triangular spaces used for closets, dressing rooms, and pantries.

The Exhibition Building reflects a transition in styles. It is octagonal in shape and features a belvedere—or lookout tower. Carpenter Gothic elements are present in the board and batten wall surface and simple eave brackets and gingerbread. The large multi-paned arched transom with its keystone is a classical element of an earlier era. Finally, the belvedere roof with its dormers is mansardic in design—the most common feature of the Second Empire style—which provides interior space within the roof area.

This focal point of the Fairgrounds complex has been altered through the years and has lost its belvedere, but it continues to serve as the significant architectural piece of the group.

SECOND EMPIRE

VICTORIA THEATER
138 NORTH MAIN STREET

Built1866; Rebuilt 1871, 1918, 1988

The Second Empire style, though it began in France as a revival style, was quickly adapted by Americans for large, formal residences. The style features a symmetrical plan of two or three stories, usually with a projecting central entry bay, and is topped by a mansard roof.

Located atop a heavy cornice, a mansard is a steep roof, flat on top, with concave or convex sides covered with decorative slate or tin. Its primary advantage is its steepness, which permits the use of the interior space including plenty of wall space for dormer windows. An additional story can be gained without the appearance of a disproportionally-sized exterior facade.

This style was popular between 1860 and 1890 and incorporated many elements of the Victorian Italianate style. Quoins, arched windows with

hoods, heavily panelled entry doors, and bracketed cornice all were commonly found on both styles.

The Victoria Theater retains much of its original character which is admirable since it has experienced two fires, a flood, and has recently undergone a major rehabilitation. While the auditorium has been remodeled, the primary facades remain essentially intact.

The building features a first story grand lobby (originally a commercial storefront), topped by symmetrical upper stories of brick with cast iron metal trim and arched multi-paned windows. A bracketed and panelled cornice supports a slate-covered mansard roof with corner bases (for missing turrets) extending above the primary roofline. A decorative central roof projection with pilasters, brackets, and a broken arched pediment is flanked by porthole dormers.

QUEEN ANNE

GEBHART-HAWKER HOUSE
338 CENTRAL AVENUE

Built c. 1880

Perhaps the most frivolous of architectural styles is the Queen Anne, 1880-1900. Its primary design theme is asymmetry. Irregular in plan, wall surfaces, roof shape and detailing make this style a major variation from prevailing styles of earlier periods.

The majority of Queen Annes were generally constructed of wood—a material readily adaptable to innumerable shapes. Decorative wood shingles added variety to wall surfaces. Ornamental carpentry, such as brackets, scrolls, vergeboards, swags, panels, finials and pendants, enriched the overall theme. Porches included elaborate cutouts or intricately designed columns, rails, and spindles.

Probably the most frequently incorporated element on a Queen Anne building

was a tower. Though most common on residential structures, towers also graced Queen Anne commercial buildings. Towers were almost as varied in design as the buildings themselves. They could be square, round, or angular in shape with conical, tent, domed or mansardic roofs.

The Gebhart-Hawker House includes both a tower and a turret which are sheathed in decorative fishscale shingles and have conical roofs. The second story of the building has fishscales, also. A front gable has gridwork panels with modillions set in each grid, and decorative scrollwork is located in the gable immediately beyond. A wide curving verandah encompasses much of the first story.

An original carriage house sits at the rear of the property.

STICK STYLE

45 WEST BABBITT STREET

Built c. 1885

As the name denotes, Stick style buildings are frame in construction with decorative board overlays called "stick work." The design is asymmetrical with interesting angles and wings highlighted with the applied stick work. Roof lines are complex and frequently feature decorative shingle patterns.

This style was popular between 1870 and 1900. It was derived from designs employing English half-timbering, applying diagonal, vertical or horizontal boards to a wall surface. By utilizing asymmetry and stick work applied solely as decoration on porches and under eaves—as well as on wall surfaces—the style became thoroughly Victorian.

Stick style detailing was incorporated into a variety of designs. It was featured on Swiss chalets, Queen Annes and, in the latter years of its popularity, on buildings with Japanese influence.

This local example of the Stick style is Victorian Queen Anne in character. It features a complex roofline and a projecting gable wing with eaves extending over a polygonal bay. This wing features carved brackets, sunbursts, and rectangular panels on the first level, and scrolls and fishscales in the upper story gable. It sports two small entry porches, one with brackets supporting a pyramidal roof. The main porch has a mansard roof supported by simple posts with a railing and square spindles. Detail is emphasized by the careful placement of color.

SHINGLE

JAMES M. COX RESIDENCE
815 WEST GRAND AVENUE

Built 1905

Characterized by the application of wood shingles to exterior wall surfaces, this style was inspired by the American colonial period. The shingles serve both decorative and functional purposes. They are the dominant design theme with other building elements taking a secondary position. Narrow eaves and windows with a minimum of trim were common. Entries were recessed.

Building shape and proportion reflected a variety of styles popular during the same period—1880-1910. Queen Annes, Colonial Revivals and Bungalows many times highlighted the visual impact of the shingles by employing them as the primary surface material.

The James M. Cox Residence is a combination of styles. It has Queen Anne shape and massing, Romanesque arches and first story stonework, and the narrow eaves minimal window trim and wood shingle surface representative of the Shingle style. The house features a central tower open on the third story with columns supporting a candle snuffer style roof. Flanking the central tower are a polygonal front bay and roof dormer and a porte cochere with stone columns.

Cox lived in the house while he was Dayton Daily News publisher. He moved from the house in 1911 and the next year began his Ohio governorship.

ROMANESQUE REVIVAL

FIRST CHURCH OF RELIGIOUS SCIENCE
11 NORTH SAINT CLAIR STREET

Built 1918

The Romanesque Revival style is characterized by the use of arches of varying sizes for window and door openings. The style was popular particularly for churches constructed between 1840 and 1900. Buildings in this style are carefully balanced, though asymmetrical.

Corner towers are another design trademark, usually projecting slightly from the face of the building. Also, they are frequently of different heights and feature different, but compatible, details. The central body of the building has a gable roof on the primary facade.

The style employs one basic masonry material with minimal trim, sometimes in another material. Restrained and dignified, the design permits the shapes within the facades to fulfill the theme.

The First Church of Religious Science features two projecting towers flanking a gable center section, the primary element of which is a massive art glass window under a Tudor arch. Entries are in the tower sections under Tudor arches, also. Limestone trim is used for accent. The towers culminate in battlements, providing a castle effect.

VICTORIAN ROMANESQUE

SACRED HEART CHURCH
45 WILKINSON STREET

Built 1888

The Victorian Romanesque style utilizes massive proportions and stone construction. Design features include round arches supported by smooth columns and windows of varying shapes and sizes. Wall surfaces exhibit more than one type and texture of stone for a polychromatic—multi-colored—effect. Popular between 1870 and 1890, this style was based on its predecessor, the Victorian Romanesque, adding increased massing and extensive use of stone.

The Sacred Heart Church incorporates

classical forms into its Victorian Romanesque design. On the primary streetface, twin towers with domed roofs supported by smooth faced columns flank a central entry wing with a pedimented gable roof. Under the pediment is a large round arch with sections of art glass. A similar wing completes the second streetface. Paired windows with red sandstone trim and similar stone banding, found throughout the building, contrast with the limestone wall surface. The most spectacular feature is the copper roofed central dome with a belvedere and porthole dormers.

RICHARDSONIAN ROMANESQUE

FIRST UNITED PRESBYTERIAN CHURCH
70 HIGH STREET

Built c. 1885

This style is named for Henry Hobson Richardson, its creator. Richardson advanced the Romanesque styles to their ultimate. His style was based almost exclusively on the monumental scale, massing, and volume he achieved. Stone, preferably red sandstone, was employed as the primary material, and details were minimal. Solidity was maintained through this restraint of detail.

The First United Presbyterian Church features a cylindrical corner tower with a flat roof which reemphasizes the broad flatness of the entire structure. The absence of eaves and combining of broad gable roofs completes the theme. Its construction in red sandstone is unique in the Dayton area.

A group of four arched windows is located over a columned recessed entry. Limestone steps are framed by sandstone handrails. Adjacent to the entry is a squat tower with a candle snuffer shaped roof.

CHATEAUESQUE

TRAXLER MANSION
42 YALE AVENUE

Built 1911

The Chateauesque is an unusual style which was popular during the early years of the twentieth century. It features flamboyant detail applied over symmetrical masonry facades. Stone and brick are combined for a polychromatic—many-colored— effect. Crowning a Chateauesque building is a steep roof, usually of tile, with projecting dormers. Structures built in this style are large and majestic; they captivate the streetscape on which they are located.

The Traxler Mansion is an elaborate Chateauesque style structure constructed of brick with stone trim. It features a recessed central entry under an iron supported glass canopy. Upper stories include balconies, a broken pedimented wall dormer, and two small bull's eye roof dormers. A porte cochere and formal Chateauesque style carriage house are located to the east of the property. Louis Traxler, the original owner, was a successful merchant with a business located in the Dayton Arcade—the West Third Street facade of which bears a resemblance to the style which he chose for his residence.

JACOBETHAN

GRACE UNITED METHODIST CHURCH
1001 HARVARD BOULEVARD

Built 1920

Jacobethan was yet another of several
styles derived from English precedents.
It was a revival style popular in England
at the turn-of-the seventeenth century
during the reigns of Elizabeth I and
James I. It was popular in America
from 1880-1930 and was the result of
architects of the nineteenth century
studying the whole of European architectural history.

The style combines in masonry the symmetry and rhythm of the Elizabethan
period with the use of interior court-
yards and ornamentation prevalent
during the Jacobean era. The style
reflects grace and majesty in a restrained
and dignified manner and exudes an
aura of spaciousness and rurality.

Repetition of details such as grouping
multi-paned, transom windows or
gabled dormers is a primary design
feature. Stone and plaster are used as
accent. Facades may be either symmetrical or asymmetrical.

Grace United Methodist Church frames
the northwest corner of Harvard Boule-
vard and Salem Avenue with its land-
scaped courtyard facing the streets. It is
a large random coursed ashlar structure,
the sanctuary of which is a street facade
slated roofed gable section with a large
round arched, transomed window, narrow copper capped octagonal bell tower
adjacent, and battlemented entry wing.
The main entry, approached by a
terraced walkway is recessed and
features large, carved wood doors under
a round arch. A secondary entry has a
similar surround and doors. Gabled
wall dormers run the length of the
sanctuary and grouped, transomed
windows frame the Disciples in glass.

A small gabled wing is more Elizabethan in design with half-timbering at the
second story. Grouped windows in
ashlar facades compose the lower story.
A small, complex roofed wing with an
end chimney is perpendicular to the secondary wing.

COMMERCIAL

MIAMI HOTEL BUILDING
SECOND AND LUDLOW STREETS

Built 1912
Lazarus Department Store

The Commercial style was popular between 1880 and 1920. Advances in building technology in the latter half of the nineteenth century coupled with the invention of the elevator enabled buildings of six to twenty stories to be constructed. These "skyscrapers" featured symmetrical building facades beginning with a traditional storefront, rising several stories in height, and culminating in heavy, overhanging cornices. Light and ventilation were primary concerns during this period, and large expanses of windows rhythmically interrupted building facades. Ornamentation was limited to repetition of an applied detail, again emphasizing the size and symmetry of the building.

BEAUX ARTS

DAYTON DAILY NEWS BUILDING
45 SOUTH LUDLOW STREET

Built 1910

The rich Beaux Arts (Bōzart) style of 1880-1920 reflected a confident America emerging from an era of rapid growth and expansion into a period of exuberant revelry and celebration. Architecture in the Beaux Arts form maintained its dignity, but incorporated a spark of imagination.

Classical forms such as columns, pedimented entries, and dentiled cornices evolved into major design elements. Colossal columns visually sustained a heavily detailed cornice. Wall surfaces blended into the background.

The Dayton Daily News building was constructed for James M. Cox, former newspaper publisher and Governor of Ohio, to emulate a bank building. Designed by local architect Albert Pretzinger, it features Roman Corinthian colossal columns flanking a slightly projecting segmental pedimented entry. An elaborate cornice boasts lion masks, scrolls, and palms among its ornamentation. The cornice is topped by a decorated parapet wall.

MISSION

FIRE STATION NUMBER 14
1422 NORTH MAIN STREET

Built 1901

The Mission style is one which incorporates the repetition of a few basic design elements into nearly any shape or floorplan. Construction is of masonry, usually stuccoed, with simple trim, and an end gable or hipped roof. Round arches, towers, tile roofs, and balconies are common.

The style was popular throughout the early twentieth century, 1890-1930. Originally, it was used in Florida and California because of the climate and vegetation in those states. By the 1920s, however, the design was being executed throughout the nation.

Fire Station #14 is an exceptional local example of the Mission style. It is a two-story brick structure with curvilin-

ear parapeted gables and a three story, pyramid roofed tower. It has a recessed second floor balcony supported by elephantine columns. Similar column treatment is found on the tower as well. Windows are multi-paned, double hung sash. Decorative gable vents are similar in style to the curves of the gables themselves. The original tile roof now is shingled.

The paired entry doors, which had been replaced by overhead vehicular doors, have been restored during the rehabilitation of the building into offices in 1988.

Station #14 was the site of the Dayton's last horse drawn fire run which occurred in 1917.

COLONIAL REVIVAL

SNEDIKER HOUSE
105 OXFORD AVENUE

Built 1905

The Colonial Revival style is unusual in that it is based on architecture from the American past. Revival houses are frequently larger than the originals and combine a variety of design elements; however, some Revival houses are authentic replicas of earlier houses and are difficult to distinguish from the originals.

The style was popular during an era, 1890-1930, when great care was used to construct solid, well-planned houses. Convenience and unpretentious grace were the dominant themes. The buildings transcended the classes with only a change in size and creation of a more elaborate interior to differentiate the upper from the middle class version.

Design elements include a central entry with a symmetrical facade, multi-paned windows—often with shutters, end chimneys, and roof dormers. The design was executed in both frame and masonry. Frequently, a sun room or porch was located at one or both ends; its roof was usually flat and railed, serving as a deck for a second story bedroom.

The Snediker House features many Colonial Revival elements. It is a brick structure with a gambrel roofline, end chimneys, and pedimented roof dormers. Under a railed full front porch with grouped Tuscan columns is a central entry with a fanlight and sidelights. An end porch complements the design of the front porch. A decorative bracketed and dentiled cornice completes the design.

BUNGALOW

106 SQUIRREL ROAD

Built c. 1915

The Bungalow style was the American favorite at the beginning of the twentieth century. The plan was easily adapted, and it became the popular style for the contractor/builder to mass-produce. The style has a few basic elements with an infinite variety of details borrowed from other styles.

Primary characteristics include one-and-one half story construction, a gabled roof with the slope facing the street, roof dormers, and front porch. Windows may be double hung sash or casement. Trim is simple and functional.

Early Bungalow houses featured floor length windows reminiscent of the Greek Revival period. Others had transoms and sidelights at the entries, details employed on Colonial Revival houses, a style popular at this time also. Many Bungalows exemplified the Craftsman ideal popular in the early twentieth century. It was a rejection of

earlier life—tastes, morals, styles, etc.—for a more natural state. Incorporating architecture into its surroundings was important.

The local representation of the Bungalow style shown above is constructed of frame with some areas stuccoed for an effective variation in texture. The story-and-a-half structure has a large shed roof, the front slope of which flairs. Double hung and casement windows are used. A full front porch has plain Tuscan columns. A porte cochere with similar columns has exposed rafters and functions as a pergola, also.

PRAIRIE

148 SQUIRREL ROAD

Built 1916

Created and molded by Frank Lloyd Wright in the early years of the twentieth century—1900-1920—the Prairie style was designed for the Midwestern landscape. Horizontality is emphasized through long building facades, wide eaves, and bands of trimwork. Wright was undoubtedly the most effective implementor of the style; however, the basics of the design were a refreshing contrast to other designs of the era and were quickly adopted and adapted.

Construction was almost exclusively in masonry, but masonry itself adapted to the style. Bricks were changed in shape, becoming longer and thinner with extremely narrow mortar joints. Trim was almost nonexistent so as not to detract from the blending of the building with the land. Shadows created by the wide, overhanging eaves further completed the natural harmony of the design.

Wright was a master, also, at redesigning and redefining interior spaces. He applied less formal and more practical concepts—the building functioned to suit the needs of its inhabitants rather than the converse, as had been the case in the past.

The local example of the Prairie style was designed by Schenk and Williams, one of Dayton's most prestigious architecture firms. It is constructed of brown brick with a stuccoed second story and has wide eaves under a series of flat hipped roof slopes. A low brick piered front porch introduces the house. A horizontal band visually separates first and second levels. Windows are a combination of double hung sash and fixed glass. Trim is virtually nonexistent, permitting the lines of the building to control the theme.

AMERICAN FOURSQUARE

M. J. GIBBONS HOUSE
22 OXFORD AVENUE

Built 1909

American Foursquares, also known as Classic Boxes, were constructed between 1900 and 1930. They are two story, hipped roofed rectangular houses. The design usually features a full front porch, roof dormers, and double hung sash windows. The simple, practical exteriors were matched by interiors with the same qualities.

Because this style was so basic and so affordable, it can be found in nearly every early twentieth century neighborhood throughout the country. Solid and substantial, the house was built to last for generations.

The M. J. Gibbons House reflects the design of the American Foursquare and highlights it with traditional details. Constructed in two-stories of blond pressed brick with a flaired hipped tile roof, the house sports an iron railed full front porch supported by pedestaled square columns. Hipped roof dormers are on each of the four roof slopes. Windows are single pane double hung sash predominantly with variety provided by the inclusion of a polygonal bay window and art and beveled glass.

Gibbons did not construct the house, but his family occupied it for twenty-five years. He is most noted locally for being responsible for the construction of the Third Street portion of the Arcade.

SPANISH REVIVAL

NIEHAUS HOUSE
1506 CATALPA DRIVE

Built c. 1925
1550 Catalpa Drive

The Spanish Revival style, popular between 1915 and 1940, provided a visual
relief to the predominant Colonial Revival style. Like the Mission style,
Spanish Revival originated in the south
and west United States but gained its
immense popularity in the Midwest.

The style is characterized by smooth
walls, hipped tile roofs, balconies, and
scrollwork. Stucco was a prevalent wall
surface. Windows were either straight
or arched, and casement units were frequently used. Large buildings included
bell towers, parapets, and decorative
plasterwork entries.

An additional feature which was to become a dominant trend in residential
construction was the use of the patio.
Relocating the primary leisure area from
the front of the house to the rear and
incorporating landscaping provided outdoor privacy.

The Niehaus House represents careful
site planning as well as attention to design details. It is a stuccoed masonry
structure with a hipped roof over the
main section. Also, it has a perpendicular wing with a gabled roof and an inset
tower, cylindrical in shape. All roofs
are tile.

Windows are a combination of straight
and arched casements. The transoms of
the arched casements and the polygonal
bay window at the end of the gable wing
have small art glass inserts. A small
bell tower straddles a portion of the
gabled wing. The entry has decorative
brick, plasterwork, and wrought iron
railings. An additional entry in the other
inset of the T has blue tile decoration.

ART DECO

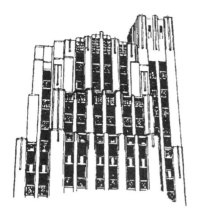

The Hulman Building is one of a few local representations of Art Deco architecture. It exemplifies all of the style's elements. Its strong, hard lines rise to stepped back stories culminating in a small corner tower. Complex linear design panels are located between vertical supports. An unusual building feature is the set of rounded windows immediately above the commercial street entry.

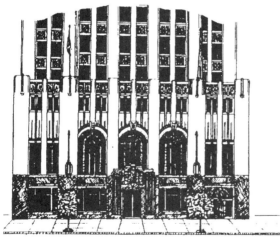

HULMAN BUILDING
120 WEST SECOND STREET

Built 1930

The most striking element of the Art Deco style is its emphasis on verticality. This strong component is softened by the use of highly decorative, filigree detail. Many Art Deco buildings are stepped back as they increase in height which breaks the verticality slightly and previews the completion of the building.

This style was used for downtown commercial buildings constructed between 1925 and 1940. It was the style of the modern skyscraper. The harshness of the vertical structural members could be downplayed with intricate and delicate designs.

ART MODERNE

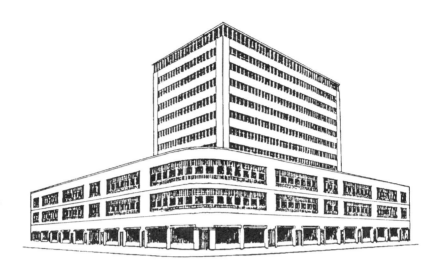

TALBOTT TOWER
131 NORTH LUDLOW STREET

Built c. 1938
Talbott Realty Building

The Art Moderne style is horizontal in nature with banding of materials, colors, and textures being employed. Curved walls with bands of windows following the building lines gave the Art Moderne style a streamlined effect. Ornamentation was present but was kept within the plan of the building and was limited to bans of ribbing or circular decoration. Construction materials were in masonry with stone, concrete, and stucco being the preferred mediums.

This style was popular between 1930 and 1945 and, to a degree, was an expansion of the earlier Art Deco style. Also, it adopted the horizontality introduced earlier by Wright and other Prairie style architects.

The Talbott Tower is a series of three buildings, the first of which is the low, three-story, curved section featuring the storefront facades. Then, the parking facilities were added. Lastly, the rectangular high-rise tower was constructed. The additions integrate into the basic design by allowing the earliest section to retain a primary role.

The first portion of the building is constructed in masonry with plain storefront sections and a corner entry comprising the first story. The upper stories feature bands of metal windows framed by glass blocks. The building curves around the corner, and the glass and wall surface follow the curve. There is no cornice, but merely a narrow horizontal band at the roofline.

STRUCTURAL
ELEMENTS

FOUNDATIONS

A foundation, as its name denotes, is the basis upon which anything is constructed. A house or similar structure rests on a masonry foundation since masonry is nearly impervious to deterioration and can sustain great weight. While a foundation is undoubtedly a structural element, it incorporates design features which correspond to the theme and style of the building.

Early construction utilized foundations made of field stone or rocks found at the site upon which the building was to be built. The stones were placed randomly to a height of about one foot. This height prevented frame building members from rotting.

By the mid-nineteenth century, local building trades had progressed sufficiently to rely on quarried limestone or soft-baked bricks for foundation materials. Though brick was used, limestone was considerably more prevalent. Dayton stone—a white, heavily veined or marbleized limestone—was favored.

As basements replaced cellars and featured windows for ventilation, coursed—or uniformly-sized—pieces of limestone became the standard. This presented a more formal, finished appearance, and a foundation began to contribute more to the overall theme of the building.

The first quarter of the twentieth century witnessed a return to simple building designs. Poured concrete replaced lime-

stone as the common foundation material because it was easier to work with and did not require repointing.

The final detail a brick or stone foundation could afford was a styled mortar joint. Commonly finished joints were flush with the foundation surface. Other styles of joints include raked (which is recessed back from the surface) and grapevine (which is convex in shape and projects outward from the foundation surface).

The most common form of deterioration in a foundation is the cracking between the stones or bricks and the subsequent crumbling of mortar in those joints. Replacing the mortar is done by repointing, a process which is described in *Exterior Walls—Masonry* section.

Serious foundation problems such as shifting or uneven settling—situations which can affect the overall stability of the structure—require some treatment which can compensate for the movement of the foundation and prohibit any further damage. Frequently, this is accomplished by pouring concrete around the footer—the portion of the foundation below ground—since the footer is usually the first area to deteriorate. It reacts to movements in the earth around the structure, particularly those resulting from weather changes.

Because foundation damage can be difficult to correct, consulting an expert trained in structural building design is advised.

Brick and stone are still available for use as foundation materials. Poured concrete and concrete block (smooth or rough-faced) are readily obtainable and most common.

For building additions, the choice of foundation materials should be guided by the foundation material of the original structure. For example, an historic structure with a limestone foundation would be complemented by an addition with a limestone, rough-faced or stuccoed foundation rather than a brick foundation. Scale and color are deciding factors.

PROHIBITIONS

Smooth faced concrete block with an above ground exposure in excess of 8"—one course—is not permitted. If smooth-faced block is desired and the exposure is greater than 8", the foundation must be stuccoed.

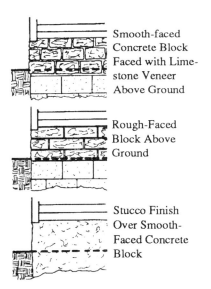

Smooth-faced Concrete Block Faced with Lime-stone Veneer Above Ground

Rough-Faced Block Above Ground

Stucco Finish Over Smooth-Faced Concrete Block

EXTERIOR WALLS

The most visible structural building element is the wall. It has the greatest amount of exposed surface and, as such, provides the initial visual impact for the building. Beyond the first desire for shelter, building walls have been a major consideration in architectural design.

Walls can be classified by materials into two primary categories. Masonry, the first category, includes brick, stone and concrete—non-combustible materials derived from minerals and inorganic substances. The second category, Frame, includes wood products and wood derivatives—materials which are flammable and based upon organic substances.

Historically, geography played a major role in the selection of building materials. Wood was abundant in the eastern United States where rich forests supplied lumber for building frames, roofs, walls, windows, doors, and trim. In the southern and southwestern sections of the country, clay was readily available and, particularly in the latter section, wood was not in abundance.

Locally, both masonry and board materials were common. Combinations of the two were found in buildings as early as the beginning of the nineteenth century.

The *Exterior Walls* section covers historical and contemporary masonry and wood materials.

MASONRY

By far, the most common masonry wall material was and continues to be brick. Techniques, however, have changed greatly. Initially, brick walls were several courses thick with interior and exterior walls sharing the building load. Brick has now assumed a decorative role, being applied as a veneer.

Primitive bricks were made at or near the construction site in wood frames. The outside or skin was baked to form a hard shell; the inside remained soft and, over time, returned to a powder. Due to the amateur nature of the process, solidity and strength varied between bricks.

Early builders used multiple thicknesses to compensate for the fluctuation within the individual members. Another variation was to use headers—bricks turned endwise. This was done within rows of stretchers—lengthwise-laid bricks—or as complete rows. With improvement in building techniques, fewer number of header rows were required.

During the last quarter of the nineteenth century, manufactured bricks were the standard. They were uniform in size and consistency. Improved technology also accounted for the development of pressed brick. This was an oil-finished brick with sharp edges and was used on

the street facade(s) of a building with the rest of the building constructed in less expensive brick.

Color experimentation began at this time, too. Brick was no longer limited to shades of red. Browns and blond complimented the stylistic return to nature. Color was used in mortar with shades matching the brick color.

The 1910's witnessed the use of texture brick, featuring raised lines or patterns. This variation was used extensively on workingmen's houses and neighborhood commercial buildings constructed prior to the Great Depression.

Limestone and sandstone were used historically as wall materials; however, limestone was more commonly found in a foundation or as trim. Both materials were favored in Romanesque style buildings which used large quarried pieces of stone.

Concrete is a rigid masonry substance composed of cement, gravel, sand, and lime. Developed in the latter half of the nineteenth century, concrete was often faced with stucco, brick, or stone. Smooth concrete walls were favored for Art Deco and Art Moderne style buildings.

Concrete block, uniformly-sized concrete pieces held together with cement mortar, is sometimes used as a replacement for poured concrete. However, exposed concrete block (as a wall surface) is not permitted; neither are artificial substances imitating stone or brick veneers although a layer of brick or stone as a facing is permitted in the construction of a new building or addition.

Stucco is a cementitous coating which can be applied over masonry, frame, or wire mesh. It provides a continuous surface which can be flat or textured. Its use was functional—to cover deterioration—or decorative.

Soft brick is susceptible to major weather changes, expanding and contracting with seasonal heat-cold exchanges. Because of this reaction, cracking or chipping of the baked surface can occur.

This damage can be repaired by removing the mortar from around a damaged brick, removing the brick, reversing it, and replacing it in the opening. This treatment provides the closest match to the surface being replaced. If the brick is seriously deteriorated, a different brick is required. New brick is readily available commercially, and innumerable varieties exist. Old brick is handled by some salvagers, as is limestone. Many times, an unnecessary and nondecorative chimney can supply needed brick. In all cases, brick should be repaired with replacement brick which matches the original in size, color, texture, and consistency.

 BRICK WITH A DAMAGED SURFACE CAN BE REMOVED, REVERSED, AND RESET INTO OPENING.

Limestone and sandstone repair is similar to that for brick. Limestone is an extremely dense substance and can withstand weather changes and impact without deteriorating. Its installation is comparable to that for brick and thus, an individual piece can be removed and replaced. Sandstone, however, is difficult to obtain due to its relative rarity as a building material.

Poured concrete's damage is due usually to cracking from uneven settling. Repair requires chipping out a v-shaped area on the face of the building, filling this area with a concrete patch, and then smoothing the surface.

Stucco is repaired somewhat similarly to concrete. The loose stucco is removed, and the underlying surface is swept clean and repaired, if necessary. As an initial coat of stucco dries, it should be dampened to prevent its drying too quickly and shrinking. A second stucco coat should be applied after a few days, and it should be gently wire brushed to give the new surface the same texture as the original. Soft stucco consists of 1 part lime, 1 part portland cement, and 5 parts sand. The top coat should have 1 part pea gravel substituted for 1 part sand.

Mortar is the "glue" which bonds individual masonry units together into a homogenous structure. Mortar, when mixed, is pliable allowing workability prior to curing to a hardened state.

Until late in the nineteenth century, mortar was composed of lime, sand, and water. The type of sand could control the color—from white to gray-brown. This mortar was referred to as soft mortar because it expanded and contracted with major weather changes. Soft mortar which is used with soft brick can be mixed by combining 1 part of portland cement with 5 parts of lime and 12-20 parts of sand. Water is added to achieve a workable consistency. Hard mortar, which should be used with limestone or hard-baked bricks, follows a similar mixture of equal parts of portland cement and lime.

Cement was developed in the late nineteenth century and was used to guarantee solidity in masonry substances. When added to mortar, a virtually unchangeable substance—hard mortar—was achieved. This worked quite well with limestone and hard-baked brick, the latter of which was developed during the same period near the turn of the twentieth century.

Color could be incorporated into the mortar through the inclusion of clay or another substance in powder form. Colored mortar added a decorative twist to a functional building element. Replacement mortar must match the original in color, composition, texture, and application in order for the joints to be unnoticeable.

Replacing deteriorated mortar is done by repointing. The process involves removing mortar to a depth of 3/4", dampening the joint, applying new mortar in the space, and smoothing the new joint with a small trowel. The new mortar joints should duplicate the original in appearance with the wet mortar being a shade darker since it will lighten as it dries. No mortar should remain on the surface of the bricks or stones between which it is applied.

TUCKPOINTING DETERIORATED MORTAR JOINT

REMOVE 3/4 INCH OF OLD MORTAR

CLEAN JOINT, THEN DAMPEN MORTAR AND BRICKS

ADD NEW MORTAR

TROWEL SHAPE TO MATCH ORIGINAL JOINT

Cleaning masonry is a process which can be an acceptable step in a repair program if the cleaning is done using non-abrasive techniques. Generally, the cleaning method should be geared to the individual surface; however, a few standards apply in the case of any historic masonry surface.

Sandblasting, featherblasting, or any similar technique which removes the outer surface of the masonry is not permitted. These abrasive methods will leave a rough, pock marked face which provides an excellent surface for new dirt to locate and which can cause walter/moisture infiltration. For soft brick or sandstone, the baked exterior can be completely removed, exposing the soft powder interior and promoting the complete deterioration of the material.

Similar problems can occur by using harsh chemicals. Hydrochloric (muriatic) acid leaves salt deposits on the building surface. These deposits can damage the surface long after the cleaning process has ended. Also, the acid most assuredly damages the soft mortar.

Some substances can be used effectively. A garden hose and bristle (never wire) brush will remove dirt. Lye and corn starch added to water is a gentle cleanser. Small percentages (four or less) of potassium chloride or hydrofluoric acid added to water and applied with a hose at no greater than 300 pounds of pressure at the nozzle (using a fan tip nozzle) is the strongest non-abrasive method permissible.

Analyze the surface prior to cleaning. Determine the type and condition of the material and the substance(s) to be removed—dirt, stains, paint. Do test patches, small areas which can be observed through several weeks of weathering. Choose the cleaning method which removes the dirt but leaves the building surface unchanged.

Efflorescence, or salt residue, may appear. This is normal after water is sprayed on masonry. It can be removed easily by scrubbing with a bristle brush and rinsing with a garden hose.

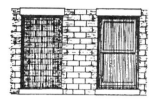

RECESSED BRICK MAINTAINS DIMENSIONS AND IMPRESSION WHERE A WINDOW HAS BEEN REMOVED

A masonry patch may be required where a building element has been altered, such as with the removal of a window. If the symmetry of the building would be interrupted by the complete elimination of the element, then the rhythm should remain intact. This can be done by recessing the patch to the location which the element occupied. Regardless of whether or not the impression is to be left in the masonry, the patch should feature materials duplicating those on the rest of the wall surface, and the rows should be aligned.

Tuck pointing or patching a masonry surface requires material of the same color, texture, composition, and application as the original.

STUCCO OVER BRICK OR STONE   SLOPPY TUCK POINTING

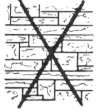

ARTIFICIAL STONE   CONCRETE BLOCK IN WINDOW OPENING

PROHIBITIONS

Because it changes the visual texture of the building, stucco or similar cement coatings are not permitted on historic masonry surfaces which have not had such materials applied previously nor are artificial substances imitating stone or brick veneers permitted. However, a layer of brick or stone as a facing is permitted in new construction if appropriate to the architecture. Exposed concrete block as a wall facing is not permitted.

Cleaning masonry by sand blasting, wire brushing, or using abrasive chemicals is prohibited.

MORE INFORMATION

"Masonry Repointing," Frederick Herman, The Old House Journal Vol. VII, No. 6, June 1979.

"Repairing Stucco," Catherine and Donald Minnery, The Old House Journal Vol. VII, No. 7, July 1979.

"Specify the Correct . . . Masonry Sealers," James G. Diedrich, American Building Restoration, Inc., The Old House Journal Vol. V, No.11, November 1975.

"Restoring Old Brickwork, " Frederick Herman, The Old House Journal Vol. III, No. 3, March 1975.

"The Case Against Removing Paint from Brick Masonry, " Theodore Prudon, The Old House Journal Vol. III, No. 2, February 1975.

"The Cleaning and Waterproof Coating of Masonry Buildings, " Robert C. Mack, Preservation Briefs 1, Washington, D.C., 1975

"Repointing Mortar Joints in Historic Brick Buildings, " Robert C. Mack, Preservation Briefs 2, Washington, D.C.

FRAME

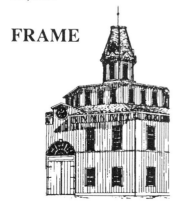

Wall surfaces made from wood were on the earliest of buildings. Simple hand hewn planks applied horizontally soon graduated to more uniform, but similarly designed, pieces—clapboards. The siding was usually lapped for better weatherization; tightly butted flush siding was used, too.

In the mid-nineteenth century, wood as a material began to be used decoratively. It was cut and sawn into numerous shapes for intricately patterned details. Wood sidings became more fanciful, and board and batten—a technique using flush vertical planks and narrow strips to cover the seams—was popularized at this time.

Differing widths of horizontal sidings, combined with vertically or diagonally laid flush boards or decorative wood shingles, were used throughout the late nineteenth and early twentieth centuries. These varying textures provided imaginative rhythm and shadow effects, and paint served to play up the variations.

Replacing damaged wood siding requires pulling the nails in the deteriorated piece, removing the piece, and replacing it with a like piece. If the new piece is a little smaller in width, the horizontal joints should be caulked.

If entire sections of siding are to be replaced, the new siding should be aligned and toothed in with the old. This is true when installing a patch where a window or door has been removed. Vertical joints should be sanded smooth and caulked. This process is aesthetically appealing and functions as a sealer.

NEW WOOD PATCH

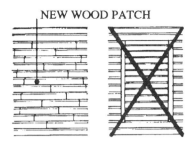

Most of the wood sidings available historically are available today. However, due to changes in lumber sizing—wood not being cut in true inches—these new sidings are approximately 1/4 to 1/2 inch narrower than previously manufactured historical materials. Careful installation is important when using new versions of siding in conjunction with existing siding.

Also available is hardboard siding which consists of pressed wood chips held together with a heat applied glue/adhesive. Hardboard is manufactured in several widths and in sheets for a board and batten effect.

PROHIBITIONS

Replacing wood siding or shingles with other than like materials is not permitted. The replacement must match in style, shape, and width to the existing.

Many wood sheathed buildings have been covered with replacement artificial sidings. These include insulbrick, asbestos block, aluminum, vinyl, and steel. While these replacements can be repaired in kind, another replacement covering cannot be added to the multiple wall sheathings if the covering is not

available. Replacement sidings are prohibited as original materials.

Wood and wood derivatives, such as hard board and masonite, are permitted with the following exceptions: reverse board and batten hardboard sheets, plywood sheets, and diagonal cedar planks.

When patching wood siding where a window or door has been removed, the vertical joints must be flush and staggered, often referred to as toothed - in. A batten strip may not be used to cover the seam.

CLAPBOARD

DROP SIDING

BOARD AND BATTEN

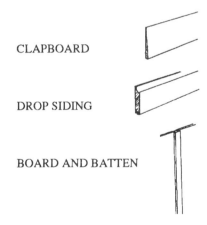

ALUMINUM

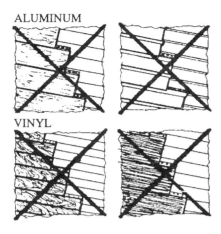

VINYL

INSULBRICK ASBESTOS BLOCK

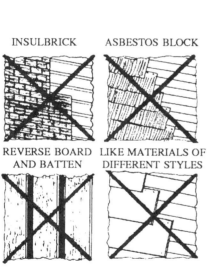

REVERSE BOARD LIKE MATERIALS OF
AND BATTEN DIFFERENT STYLES

ROOFS

As with any structural building element, a roof serves a functional purpose initially with its design aspects taking a secondary role. Wood shingles over a gabled or pitched style roof was a prevalent feature until well past the middle of the nineteenth century. Other early styles were gambrel, hip, and pyramid.

All of the early styles had one element in common: no valleys or low areas where water would concentrate. The roof slopes were uninterrupted so that water would be eliminated before it could deteriorate the wood shingle surface.

As building styles became more imaginative and technology advanced, roof designs became more complex. These roofs combined simpler slopes with more integral design elements.

Queen Anne style structures, for example, nearly always included a tower or turret which had an angled or domed roof.

Wood shingles were eventually replaced by slate tiles or sheet metal. Both materials could withstand repeated weather changes and added interest to

the building. Slate, in particular, was used during the late nineteenth century and was applied in a variety of shapes and patterns. Less common were tin or copper shingles.

During the Victorian era of the mid to late nineteenth century, metal ornamentation was applied to roof ridges. Widows' walks—lookouts atop a flat section of roofing—included iron cresting, decorative metal work which gave the appearance of a low railing. Many a Queen Anne's tower had a cap or finial.

TOWER

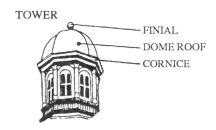

FINIAL
DOME ROOF
CORNICE

Skylights were introduced in the late nineteenth century, also. They provided light and aesthetic interest to a building's interior in a manner previously unavailable. These lights were mounted flush into the roofs and had wood or metal frames.

The turn of the twentieth century brought a return to simple, practical building designs with functional roofing materials. Clay tile was favored due to its textural interest and durability. Asphalt and asbestos shingles began to be used, although their major importance came later following further technological progress.

Both a roof's shape and its material had become integrated into a building's overall design theme, making the roof a significant style element.

Roofs of most historic buildings were constructed over rafters—supports which defined the shape of the roof and were tied into the building walls; some were constructed with additional trusses. Trusses are rafters with additional cross supports to better withstand the weight of the roof's surface. Because not all buildings have these additional supports, no more than three layers of roofing surface materials—tiles or shingles—are permitted.

If a fourth layer of roofing is necessary, the first three must be removed. Once this is accomplished, the roof rafters or trusses can be examined. Also, roof sheathing may need to be replaced. Sheathing consists of wood strips—now plywood sheets—placed across the rafters or trusses to which the shingles are nailed.

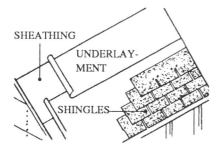

SHEATHING

UNDERLAY-MENT

SHINGLES

Three-in-one shingles are manufactured in strips which are overlapped and held in place with nails. The exposed part of the shingle may be uniformly rectangular or vary minimally in size and shape, giving the appearance of wood shingles. French lock shingles are individual diamond-shaped pieces which interlock. These strips can be removed and replaced individually.

Slate, a common historic roofing material, requires careful repair. The existing slate should never be walked on as the pieces are brittle and will crack easily. Walking should be done only along the roof valleys with soft soled shoes. Repair requires an L-shaped ladder placed across a roof ridge to evenly distribute the weight of the roofer. A damaged piece of slate can be replaced by inserting a slate nail cutter under the piece, clipping the nails, and removing the slate tile. A metal tab is slid under the intact shingles immediately above the area where replacement is being made. The tab is then nailed down. A new shingle is laid over it, but under the other slates, and the tab is bent up and over the new slate tile, holding it in place.

Other damage to a slate roof may be the result of rusted nails although this is an infrequent problem. Correcting this requires removal of the slate roof and reattaching the slate pieces with slating nails carefully so as to not drive them in too tightly into the slate.

Tile is a substantial roof material but can be easily damaged by direct pressure. A fallen tree limb striking a tile roof can cause cracking or breaking of the tiles. Repair of tile roofing is similar to slate. Both share the same problems of damaged pieces or rusted nails, and neither should be walked on. Individual replacement of pieces is usually much less expensive than removal of the surface and replacement with modern shingles.

Sheet metal's damage is due to corrosion, fostered by weather exposure. Acids carried through the air or present in rain can initiate the corrosion process. However, keeping the surface painted should prevent this damage.

Undoubtedly, the most common roofing problem is damaged flashing. Since it is found in all of the joints—the most common areas for water damage—flashing must be maintained, and it should be covered by a minimum of four inches (4") of roofing material. Also, it should be painted with a metal preservative, the most popular of which is "roofer's red."

Asphalt and fiberglass shingles are the most commonly available roofing materials. Slate and clay tile are available, although installation is more difficult. Standing seam sheet metal, including copper, may be used though it was much less common historically.

Flat roofs require single membrane roofs, such as tar and gravel, sheet metal with flush seams, or fiberglass sheeting. A wood deck can be constructed over the roof if it is to serve as the floor for a second story balcony. Fiberglass sheeting is quite satisfactory as a deck covering, also.

Flashing is available in metal sheets, the most common being tin or aluminum. Copper is also available. Flashing other than copper should be painted black, red, or the roof color.

Skylights are quite popular in a variety of sizes and shapes. They can be of clear or bronze tinted glass with wood or metal frames, flush mounted on non-streetside elevations.

PROHIBITIONS

Aluminum or plastic roofing is prohibited as is rolled roofing. Neither type adds to the design, character, or significance of a historic structure. The first type is an attempt to imitate wood shingles. The second type is a material with a short period of effectiveness.

FRENCH LOCK SHINGLES
GABLE ROOF

SLATE SHINGLES
MANSARD ROOF

STANDING SEAM SHEET METAL
HIPPED ROOF
CONICAL TOWER

Shingle colors should be medium to dark, preferably shades of black, brown, or gray; also permitted in some cases are green or red. The last two colors are appropriate to late nineteenth and early twentieth century buildings only. White or light gray roofing or a shingle with white in it is prohibited.

Three-in-one tab or French lock shingles are appropriate. Unexaggerated asphalt or fiberglass shake shingles are permitted.

Every effort should be made to repair rather than replace slate or clay tile roofing because these are significant building elements.

Removal of ornamental ridge caps, cresting, or roof finials is prohibited. These items are metal and must be painted with a metal preserving paint. Red is historically accurate for historic roof metal other than cresting—which should be painted black. If roof vents are installed, they must be painted to match the roof color.

No more than three layers of shingles are permitted on a roof. Removal of the existing roofing is required if the top of the three layers merits replacement.

Removal of decorative fascia or soffit is prohibited. Continuous aluminum sheeting with baked color finish or painted to match the trim color(s) is permitted in place of an unadorned fascia and soffit. It must have flush seams and run parallel with the building. Perpendicular or ridged aluminum is prohibited.

Bubble or flush mounted skylights are permitted. The frames must be bronze or painted the roof color and should not be located on a prominent roof slope.

FOR MORE INFORMATION

"Roofing for Historic Buildings," Sarah M. Sweetser, Preservation Briefs 4, Washington, D.C., 1978.

"Roofing with Wood Shingles," C. R. Meyer, The Old House Journal Vol. I, No. 1, October 1973.

"Flat-Roof Repairs," The Old House Journal Vol. I, No. 1, October 1973.

"Roofing: Repair or Replacement?" R. A. Clem Labine, The Old House Journal Vol. IX, No. 2, February 1981.

"Repairing Slate Roofs," R. A. Clem Labine, The Old House Journal Vol. III, No. 12, December 1975.

CHIMNEYS & FLUES

Historically, a chimney is a chute for smoke, fumes, and heat from a fireplace or furnace, thereby serving as an integral part of a structure. In addition to its function, a chimney frequently acts as a design element, incorporating unusual brick patterns and details. Also, some featured embellishments such as chimney caps and pots which improved heat production and reduced drafts in the fireplace.

Masonry chimneys can be a source of leaks if either the cap at the top or the flashing at the base has deteriorated. Cracking mortar joints can emit water, loosening and eroding bricks. In extreme cases, a chimney can crumble or lean and require rebuilding. Unused

chimneys should be repaired and capped. This eliminates drafts, reduces deterioration, and maintains a chimney's important decorative role. Furthermore, retention of the chimney permits future operation of its fireplace(s).

Chimneys serving operating fireplaces or furnaces should be cleaned regularly. The flue must not become blocked or lined with residue, either of which could contribute to a fire. Old flues were originally lined with mortar instead of tile. If mortar is deteriorating and dropping down the flue, this lining is probably no longer protecting the chimney brick from the fire's hot exhaust. Metal or ceramic pipe is available in a variety of diameters to line flues. Lining the flue will protect original bricks and mortar while still allowing fireplace usage.

LINING FLUE WITH
METAL PIPE

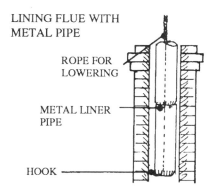

ROPE FOR
LOWERING

METAL LINER
PIPE

HOOK

CHIMNEY
FLUE
FLASHING
ROOF

FLUE LINING

Unpainted chimney brick should not be painted. Furthermore, chimneys should not be stuccoed as a means of repair. The great temperature differences which a chimney experiences will crack a stucco coating and eliminate its effectiveness.

New chimneys built for old or new fireplaces should be of the same material and design as existing, original chimneys. Details and proportions should be similar to existing chimneys.

In addition to masonry chimneys, metal stacks boxed with wood and painted are appropriate. A metal and wood chimney must maintain the proportions of a masonry chimney and reflect the design of the structure to which it is attached.

Stovepipes accompanying wood stoves shall be treated as metal chimneys. The exception to this requirement is a stovepipe located on a one story house and protruding 3' or less through the addition's roof. A raw stovepipe of this type must be painted a dark brown, green, gray, or black corresponding to the roof color.

Chimney pots handcrafted from fired terra cotta clay in historically accurate designs are readily available. Less common chimney caps are obtainable.

PROHIBITIONS

Destroying the stylistic contribution of chimneys is prohibited. Removal of chimneys may be permitted if the chimney does not contribute architecturally to the building. Imitation stone or brick and metal formed to look like stone or brick are not permitted, and fake or false chimneys and flues may not be added to a structure. Unsheathed stovepipes or metal chimneys are prohibited on primary structures or visible facades.

FOR MORE INFORMATION

"Repairing Old Chimneys," Matt Huff, The Clean Sweep, The Old House Journal Vol. V, No. 5, May 1977.

"Chimney Sweeping," Eva Horton, Kristia Associates, The Old House Journal Vol. VI, No. 8, August 1978.

STYLE
ELEMENTS

DOORS

Historically, the front door of a structure was a prominent element of the facade. Doors crafted from fine woods resplendent with decorative glass and elegant hardware expressed an owner's taste, character, and wealth. Doors were constructed of a solid wood frame inset with panels of glass or wood that were held in place by moldings. This configuration created a handsome three dimensional design. Front doors were often part of a carefully coordinated entrance incorporating decorative cornices, pilasters, sidelights, stairs, railings, balusters, and in the case of commercial buildings, lighting, signage, and shop windows. Rear and side doors were usually less elaborate in design and detail reflecting their service and delivery functions, but were sympathetic in style.

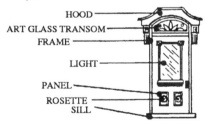

HOOD
ART GLASS TRANSOM
FRAME
LIGHT
PANEL
ROSETTE
SILL

Original doors and entrances, because of their high visibility and prominence, are important components of a structure; every effort should be made to retain, restore, and protect them. Desirable features include original or period hardware, unpainted stone sills and lintels, hood molds, transoms, and wood or metal architraves.

Late nineteenth century doors were often embellished with etched, leaded,

stained or beveled glass panels. If the glass is chipped, cracked or missing, it can be repaired or replaced with new glass. Fancy glass of similar style can often be purchased from antique or glass dealers.

An exterior wood door is continually exposed to the deteriorating effects of sun, wind, moisture, and customer usage. It requires a protective coating of either paint or exterior use varnish. A door in good condition is easy to maintain, requiring a light application of new coats of varnish or paint. An extensively damaged finish requires complete sanding or paint removal prior to refinishing.

Storm doors should also be considered for their decorative abilities as well as their energy conservation and protective properties. See also *Weatherproofing* and *Home Security*.

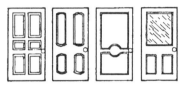

Multi-panelled doors of wood or steel with or without glass are readily available as are fancy glass originals and reproductions. Brass, porcelain, and wood hardware add to the character of the door.

PROHIBITIONS

The replacement door must fit the existing opening, with the opening being neither decreased nor enlarged in size. Flush steel or flush wood doors and interior doors used on the exterior are prohibited.

WINDOWS

Windows make an important contribution to the character of a building and the block. Size, shape, type, ornamentation, and orientation reflect building style, and rhythm created by the placement of windows symmetrically or asymmetrically enhances the style.

Historically, windows served as a functional means of providing light and air circulation within a building. A storefront window also functioned as a display area for the store's wares. The development of the glass making process provided for larger panes (or lights) with a variety of hues and textures. During the Victorian era, glass making graduated to a fine art. Fancy bevelled, leaded, etched, curved, and art (stained) glass embellished many buildings.

Except for the plate glass of the storefront, double hung sash is the most common window type. This window has two vertically-movable sections (sash) set in one frame and can feature one or several panes per sash.

A common window is an open ended box set through a wall. The bottom of the box, or sill, is of heavier stock and slopes away from the wall to shed water. The three remaining sides constitute the jamb with the two vertical sections further classified as stiles. The sash is the wooden frame which holds the glass. A double hung window has two sash frames which travel in the stiles. These sash frames are hung on pulleys by weighted cords.

After several coats of paint have been applied to a window over the years, the space between sash and frame can become clogged and impede movement.

COMMON SASH ARRANGEMENTS

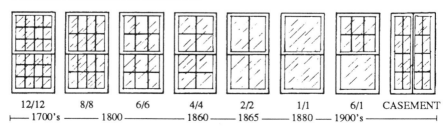

| 12/12 | 8/8 | 6/6 | 4/4 | 2/2 | 1/1 | 6/1 | CASEMENT |

├──── 1700's ──── 1800 ──────── 1860 ──── 1865 ──── 1880 ── 1900's ────┤

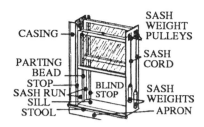

CASING — SASH WEIGHT PULLEYS
PARTING BEAD — SASH CORD
STOP — BLIND STOP
SASH RUN —
SILL — SASH WEIGHTS
STOOL — APRON

Window fabrication must be of wood—although the exterior face can feature a vinyl cladding. Vinyl or aluminum replacement windows are prohibited. Any desired size or shape can be reproduced, and glass types such as etched or bevelled are readily available.

ETCHED GLASS PATTERNS

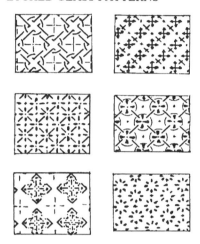

A flat tool will break the paint seal. Missing, broken, or frayed sash cords can be replaced by removing interior window casing, thereby getting access to the weight pocket. Cotton rope with a nylon center and labeled as sash cord is an appropriate new cord material. Flat steel chain can also be used.

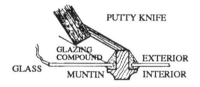

PUTTY KNIFE
GLAZING COMPOUND
GLASS
MUNTIN
EXTERIOR
INTERIOR

If the putty seal securing glass within a sash has cracked or the glass requires replacement, the existing sealing material must be removed. Before replacing the glass, owners should consult local housing/building code officials to ensure the use of proper glass. Glazing compound can be applied to the newly set glass within its frame, and the compound can be smoothed with a putty knife. Painting will further seal the window pane edges.

Skylights are windows set through a roof. They originated in the late nineteenth century on a small scale. Recently, skylights have become extremely popular. They come in a wide variety of dimensions, are framed with wood or aluminum, and feature bubbled or flat glass. The low profile style of skylights are preferred to the bubble style because of their minimal visibility. If aluminum frames are desired, they must be bronze in color. Skylights are appropriate where they do not have prominent street visibility.

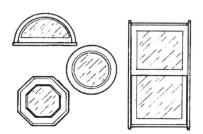

GREEN HOUSE WINDOW FOR SIDE AND REAR FACADES ONLY

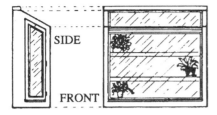

A relatively recent product is the thermal pane window. This utilizes from two to four panes of glass placed in the same frame with seals between the glass pieces. To provide the appearance of multiple panes per sash with the use of these windows, snap-in interior muntins are available. Respect should be given to the style of the structure when pane configuration is considered. If repair of a thermal pane window is required, factory exchange of the damaged sash is necessary.

PROHIBITIONS

A replacement window must be of the same material, size, proportion, style, and configuration as an original window. Vinyl or aluminum replacement windows are prohibited. When replacing windows, caution must be taken to insure that the frame and sash combination does not reduce dramatically the glass area of the window. This will change the fenestration of the building. Window openings cannot be reduced to accommodate new windows. The pane configuration must match the original configuration of the windows being replaced so as not to alter the character of the building. Raw aluminum, other metal finishes, and tinted or mirrored glazing are not permitted. Aluminum storm windows are permitted only if painted or vinyl-clad.

FOR MORE INFORMATION

"Fixing Double Hung Windows," James McConkey, The Old House Journal Vol. VII, No. 12, December 1979.

"Restoring Rotted Widow Sills," The Old House Journal Vol. II, No. 8, August 1974.

"Defeating Decay," Clem Labine, The Old House Journal Vol. IX, No. 5, May 1981.

"Make Your Own Ornamental Wood Screens," Susan Clark, The Old House Journal Vol. IX, No. 7, July 1981.

"Window Glass," H. Weber Wilson, The Old House Journal Vol. VI, No. 4, April 1978.

"Your Residential Stained Glass," H. Weber Wilson, Architectural Ecology, Chambersburg, Pa.

Special Window Issue, The Old House Journal Vol. X, No.4, April 1982.

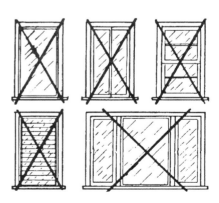

PORCHES

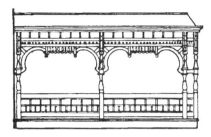

Porches originated from the classic Greek portico which defined the entrance to a structure with an elaborate framing element. Incorporating columns, pediment, and often a grand stair, the portico was designed as an impressive introduction to the interior living space.

The mid-nineteenth century experienced a romanticism in building design. Nature and geography influenced the size and shape of a building, thus achieving a composite whole, and a verandah became an integral element in this design.

The porch and verandah satisfied human needs on three levels. Emotionally, the porch served as a transition between the natural and man-made environments. Creativity was expressed through architectural embellishments such as columns, brackets, scrollwork, and spindles. The verandah provided an opportunity for enhancement of a structure's basic theme.

PORTICO

Functionally, a properly designed and oriented porch dramatically reduced heat gain in the summer months. In winter, low angled sun rays entered house windows to warm the room. The verandah often linked major entrances with minor ones, shielding these entrances from weather. A broad verandah provided a living area that was cooled by breezes. The Victorian verandah featured wicker and folding canvas furniture, plants, straw mats, and canvas awnings or blinds. The porch swing was also a common feature.

Socially, the front porch offered a place for the residents of a house to recognize or ignore passersby. Casual acquaintances and neighbors could be entertained here without the personal commitment of the formal parlor. Thus, the porch served as a connection to the neighborhood.

PORTE COCHERE

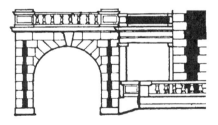

Porches are focal points of a facade and deserve proper rehabilitation. If rebuilding is required, duplication or reuse of existing decorative details is important. Recycling trim insures retention of original character.

Floor boards on wood porches receive substantial wear and tear. These interlocking boards can be turned over if the top side is worn. Rotted boards can be replaced with new boards treated with a wood preservative. Porch floors were originally painted grey, beige, brown, or dark green; this continues to be the standard.

For structures built during the early years of the twentieth century, poured concrete was used as a porch floor material. Concrete is fairly impervious but is susceptible to settling cracks. New concrete can be poured after the damaged material is chipped out. The porch can be colored the original gray or painted gray, beige, brown, or dark green.

Columns are necessary structural and decorative elements; therefore, their preservation is extremely important. Deterioration of columns will cause collapse of the porch roof. Rotted wood columns can be reproduced, or sections can be duplicated and grafted to the original.

Railings and balusters function as protective supports for persons utilizing the porch and must be able to bear a person sitting on or leaning against them. They also enhance the design style of the porch. Repair of a railing is similar to that of a column—duplication of parts or reproduction of the whole.

The late nineteenth and early twentieth centuries witnessed the use of heavily decorative cast iron work on porches as supports and railings. Pieces can be rewelded or duplicated and then primed and painted. Also introduced during this period was the use of stone column bases. This was common particularly if the house had a raised foundation. Due to the size and weight of the materials, repairs such as resetting stone require professionals.

Due to a porch's constant exposure to the elements, wood should be constructed of treated lumber which must weather for approximately one year prior to painting. This prolongs the life of the members and discourages deterioration. Lumber can be treated on-site or at a lumber yard. Treated lumber should be allowed to cure for a period of time. Depending upon the type of treatment, a few weeks to several months may be required.

Exterior steps receive constant wear from foot traffic and weather. Stone, concrete, brick, and wood steps all require proper maintenance for durability. Wood steps are particularly prone to damage. The greatest source of wood step problems is poor drainage. Worn treads with depressions in the middle pool water which will saturate and rot exposed wood. The easiest solution to this is to turn over the worn treads if possible.

Many porches, especially on Victorian homes, had latticework between the porch floor and the ground. Replacement latticework is available commercially or can be easily constructed. Commercial latticework needs to be framed prior to its installation on porches but may not be used to enclose porches for privacy.

LATTICE PANEL CONSTRUCTION

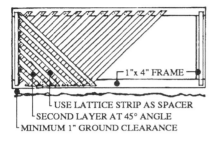

1"x 4" FRAME

USE LATTICE STRIP AS SPACER
SECOND LAYER AT 45° ANGLE
MINIMUM 1" GROUND CLEARANCE

MOUNTING PANEL TO PORCH POSTS

TOP VIEW

LATTICE PANEL
PORCH POST
TRIM BOARDS

A wood preservative and primer should be applied to all surfaces before assembly. A minimum of one-inch ground clearance needs to be allowed to reduce chances of rot and insect infestation.

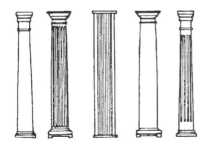

Many products are available which duplicate original floor boards, balusters, columns, and railings enabling retention of original materials and character. Wood columns in a variety of styles, heights, and diameters can be ordered from lumber companies. Steel columns are available, and decorative column caps and cornice work are reproducible.

PROHIBITIONS

Porches and steps which are appropriate to the building and its development should be maintained. Distinguishing architectural features of wood, iron, cast iron, and stone should be restored or duplicated and not removed. A new porch should be of similar architectural style, character, and material as the principal structure on which it is to be located. No aluminum or vinyl porch enclosures are permitted. Rear porches may be screened or glass enclosed; however, the proportions of the porch must be maintained. Porch roofing material should match the color and texture of the main roofing material. Lightweight aluminum designed as "ornamental iron" metal supports and rails are inappropriate and shall not be used. Unnatural floor coverings, such as indoor-outdoor carpeting, and pre-cast concrete steps are not permitted.

APPROPRIATE PORCH SCREENING

ORNAMENTATION

RECESSED PANELS
GRID WORK WITH MEDALLION CENTERS
CANTILEVERED TURRET
FISHSCALES SKIRT
RECESSED PANELS
FINIAL
CAP
FRIEZE BAND
DENTILS
CORNICE PANEL

Ornamentation, combining a variety of materials, patterns, and techniques, is the most interesting and unique architectural element a building can feature. Such imaginative artistic details add personality.

Early ornamentation reflected the skill and imagination of the carpenter. Wood was sawed, chiseled, turned, or sculpted into an endless variety of designs and uses. Bargeboards, brackets, balusters, sunburst, capitals, dentils, cornices, pendants, finials, posts, pilasters, and columns served decorative and sometimes functional purposes. Wood shingles, prevalent as a siding element in the late nineteenth century, incorporated a decorative flair with the introduction of such patterns as

fishscales, sawtooth, diamond, square, scalloped, and diagonal which could be layered to form an infinite choice of designs.

Brick and stone also were used to create visual interest on a building. Though not as versatile as wood, they were more durable and easier to maintain. Brick detailing was achieved by projection or recession along the horizontal course. Shadows on the building reflected the three dimensionality. Stone as the most common masonry detail material was used for columns, capitals, pediments, arches, and quoins.

Metal provided a more workable, lightweight material satisfying a need to produce finely detailed ornaments. It

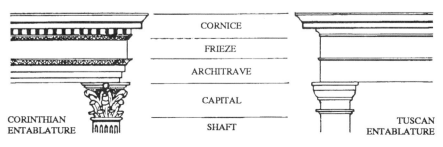

CORINTHIAN ENTABLATURE

CORNICE
FRIEZE
ARCHITRAVE
CAPITAL
SHAFT

TUSCAN ENTABLATURE

was available in flat, sheet, and solid cast forms. The former could be bent, shaped, and stamped into a variety of trims, cornices, arches, and pediments. Iron could be cast into solid engravings or delicate filigree cresting.

Plaster was used ornamentally during the late nineteenth century. Molds guaranteed the exactness of hardened plaster forms, achieving duplicity found with iron in a light-weight material impervious to rust.

Ornamentation took a variety of forms fabricated from numerous materials: wood, stone, brick, metal, and plaster, all of which provide visual interest and enhance a building's style. These elements make an important contribution to a building's historical significance.

Wood and plaster pieces are easy to reproduce. Sections can be reattached, sealed, and painted. Cracks in wood can be filled with a flexible caulking which will expand and contract with the weather variations as does the wood.

Metal trim damage is often limited to rust which can be sanded and painted with a metal primer and a rust inhibiting paint. Dents in sheet metal can be pulled or popped out; holes can be patched with fiberglass or metal.

The easiest means of repairing damaged brick detailing is to chip out mortar around the damaged brick, remove the brick, reverse it, and return it to the original location. Should the damage be too excessive, a brick of similar color, texture, and size should be used. If another area of the building, such as a chimney, requires rebuilding, bricks may become available which could be used for detail.

Stone is the least frequently damaged ornamentation material and the most difficult to repair. Due to its weight and the skill needed to duplicate a design, a professional stone mason usually is required. If the detail piece is a plain lintel or similar common unadorned piece of stonework, materials are readily available, and repair is manageable.

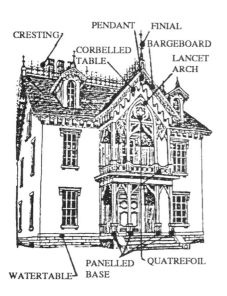

CRESTING
PENDANT   FINIAL
BARGEBOARD
CORBELLED
TABLE
LANCET
ARCH
WATERTABLE
PANELLED
BASE
QUATREFOIL

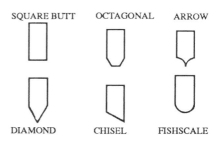

SQUARE BUTT   OCTAGONAL   ARROW

DIAMOND   CHISEL   FISHSCALE

Ornamentation elements can be reproduced. Availability, execution, and installation varies with type of material and complexity of the design. Wood, as the most commonly used trim material, is easiest to reproduce and install.

REPRODUCTIONS AVAILABLE

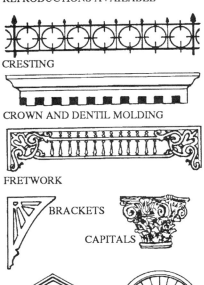

CRESTING

CROWN AND DENTIL MOLDING

FRETWORK

BRACKETS

CAPITALS

PEDIMENTED
WINDOW HOOD

SUNBURST

FOR MORE INFORMATION

"Sawn Wood Ornamentation," Carolyn Flaherty, The Old House Journal Vol. II, No. 7, July 1974.

Ben Karp, Ornamental Carpentry on Nineteenth-Century American Houses, New York: Dover Publications, 1981.

PROHIBITIONS

Original ornamentation should not be removed, altered, or destroyed. However, detailing of a similar style and type—sharing the same time period as the structure or original decoration—can be used to replace original ornamentation. Vinyl and aluminum details are prohibited.

PAINT

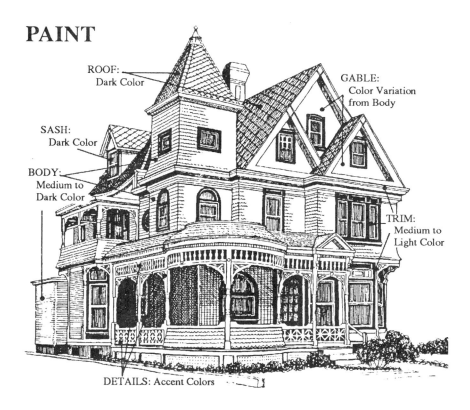

ROOF:
Dark Color

GABLE:
Color Variation
from Body

SASH:
Dark Color

BODY:
Medium to
Dark Color

TRIM:
Medium to
Light Color

DETAILS: Accent Colors

Color, through the use of paint, is one of the most important style elements of a building. This medium affords an opportunity for creative expression and accentuation of decorative details and is the one vehicle that both establishes and reflects the personality of building and owner. Visually, fresh paint will make the greatest impact in a rehabilitation project.

Furthermore, paint is a necessary protective element—a renewable skin. This coating is applied over wood, masonry, and metal facade elements, including walls, windows, doors, and trim. Paint seals and protects these components from weather damage.

Color selection influences the character of a neighborhood just as it affects the appearance of a particular building.

Blending colors with nearby buildings is as significant as choosing compatible colors for an individual building. Color intensity should enhance features and reinforce the structural and stylistic elements of a building.

Early building styles in America emulated noble Greek and Roman prototypes in Europe; however, construction was executed in local materials. Frame was the common medium which could be painted a stone color (white, beige, or gray) , and texture could be achieved by adding sand to the paint mix.

The mid-nineteenth century witnessed the development of two contrasting color themes. Gothic buildings employed picturesque details with nature as a backdrop. Earthy tones of grays, yellows, and tans created harmony between architecture and landscape.

During the same era, building details became more creative, and popularity of these details increased. Darker colors were used throughout a building, but detail emphasis was achieved through the use of vivid contrasts by not limiting the painting of trim elements to darker shades of the primary colors; new colors were introduced to the palette.

The late years of the nineteenth century witnessed a less vibrant use of contrasting colors and a darkening of the overall scheme. Trim details were at the height of popularity, but due to their intricacy had no need to rely on color for accentuation.

A reinstitution of classical architecture occurred at the turn of the twentieth century. Simple, pastel color schemes returned to fashion, presenting a solid forthright impression.

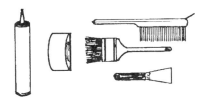

The protective coating that paint provides depends upon proper application and maintenance. A deteriorated paint surface can be both unsightly and physically damaging. Neglected maintenance of a painted surface is the most obvious rehabilitation problem and one requiring care and attention to correct.

Most paint problems are the result of

one or more of the following factors: poor surface preparation, moisture contact, and inferior quality materials. Proper surface preparation is usually the key to insure paint durability. Paint will adhere only to a dull, dry, clean, firm, sealed, and primed surface.

All loose paint on the original surface should be scraped. A sanding block or orbital sander will provide an even level surface on which new paint can adhere. Washing the surface with tri-sodium-phosphate (TSP) or other cleaner will remove all chalk, powder, and mildew which adversely affect paint adhesion. To further protect subsurface material and prolong paint life, all cracks should be filled with a caulking; loose sections should be resecured.

Thorough surface preparations should be followed with a coat of a high-quality oil based primer/sealer. This coating will restore oil to weathered materials, seal porous surfaces, and provide a uniform film conducive to finish coat adhesion. The primer/sealer should dry completely prior to painting.

Often the paint surface is merely dirty and requires a simple washing with a mild detergent and water solution. This will prolong the life and appearance of the paint without adding excessive coatings.

No paint should be applied to damp material. Durability is shortened considerably when materials to be painted are not dry. The primer/sealer coat should be allowed to dry thoroughly. Water on a existing painted surface or absorbed into a wood subsurface should evaporate completely prior to painting. Generally, a surface should only be repainted when trouble signs appear. These are alligatoring, checking, excessive chalking, blistering and peeling, or exposed material. Often, only a small area or section will require surface repair, preparation, and new coating.

The following sections outline specific problem areas for wood, masonry, and metal painted surfaces. It is important to understand and correct the cause of a problem in order for any new coating to perform properly. *Wood, Masonry,* and *Metal* sections identify specific causes and cures for common problems affecting paint durability on each material.

WOOD

Wood, an organic (once living) material, is the most susceptible building product to decay when exposed to the elements. Therefore, wood should be covered with some sort of protective coating. Maintenance of this coating can be complicated by factors inherent in the paint, material, or building.

The failure of paint on wood is almost always a problem of adhesion, generally attributable to poor surface preparation or moisture contact.

Alligatoring

Alligatoring or scale pattern cracks in the paint film are often caused by the inability of the top coat to bond smoothly to a glossy coat beneath. The problem is compounded further when many coats of paint have been applied to wood. Excessive coatings inhibit paint elasticity. Thus, failure results as wood continues to expand and contract due to temperature and humidity changes.

An effective solution to this problem is removal of all old paint in affected areas by scraping and sanding or by use of a paint stripping compound. This treatment should be followed by primer and finishing coats.

Checking

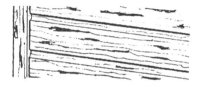

Checking of paint—characterized by a pattern of short, narrow breaks in the top layer of the coating—is also caused by a loss in film elasticity. These breaks generally follow the grain line of the wood subsurface.

In this case, loose paint should be removed with a scraper and wire brush. Exterior spackle can be used to fill depressions between paint which is firm and cannot be removed by scraping and sanding. Then the entire surface should be washed with TSP or another cleanser, primed, and painted.

Excessive Chalking

It is normal for all painted surfaces to chalk to some degree. Normal chalking is the result of sun and moisture slowly "weathering" the film surface. However, excessive formation of fine powder on the surface of a paint film is not normal. Excessive chalking is caused by failure to adequately prime and seal a porous surface, spreading surface coats too thin, or overthinning of paint. Often, paint is stored on a cold concrete floor in a basement or garage. A common mistake is to thin this "thick" cold paint. Instead, the paint container should be warmed in water, placed in the sun, or on a heating register until the coating reaches a normal stirring consistency.

To solve the problem of excessive chalking, the chalk residue must be removed. The process includes washing the area with a stiff brush and a TSP solution to loosen deteriorating material and rinsing with spray from a garden hose to remove film. Once the surface is dry, a coat of primer will uniformly seal the surface and provide a good medium to which finishing coats can bond.

If chalk has stained adjacent brick or stone, the stains can be scrubbed with a stiff brush and detergent solution. If the brick is a slightly lighter color after it dries, it can be masked by rubbing a piece of brick over the area.

Blistering

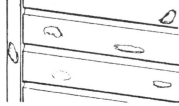

Blisters can be caused by heat, moisture, or both. If a top coat is applied in direct sunlight, heat blisters can result. The film dries too quickly, and trapped solvents later vaporize, causing pressure against the top coat. This problem is especially common when dark, heat absorbing colors are used. Furthermore, moisture trapped in or behind paint film will vaporize or "perculate" when exposed to the sun. The resulting pressures also will cause blistering.

Blisters should be removed by scraping and sanding. If the blister was caused by moisture, the source must be removed. Blistering is usually the beginning stage of peeling; correction of moisture problems is covered in the next section.

Peeling

Peeling is the common paint problem which results when wet wood swells under paint, causing the paint film to loosen, crack, and chip away. Uncaulked joints allow moisture to seep into adjoining wood surfaces. Caulking in a deteriorated condition will have the same effect. Other ways water can reach painted wood include clogged, overflowing gutters; damp basements; boards located too near bare ground; and painting over wood damp with rain or mildew.

Often, the most common failure of paint due to moisture is the result of water vapor becoming trapped within exterior walls. Condensation from washing, cooking, and bathing passes from interior rooms into the exterior wall cavity. Without adequate ventilation, the moisture will condense on the back of exterior wall material, dampening the wood.

Moisture is frequently responsible for paint failure. Every step possible should be taken to eliminate moisture contact on wood. Joint areas—such as window sash and frame—should be carefully inspected. Loose or cracked caulking should be replaced with a high quality flexible product; a compound that will expand and contract as wood swells and shrinks is necessary.

Exhaust vents should be installed and used to relieve moisture in kitchen, bathroom, and laundry areas. Dishwashers and dryers should have individual vents. Exterior walls around such high moisture rooms or adjacent to drains, pipes, radiators, or heating ducts may require a small three-quarter inch (3/4") diameter vent plug installed two inches (2") above floor level. This will allow moisture laden air to escape. These plugs must be painted the color of surrounding material.

A vapor barrier can be established to eliminate moisture from travelling into the exterior wall cavity from an interior wall surface. This can be accomplished by installing insulation with a foil vapor barrier in the wall cavity or by use of a fiberglass and resin interior wall covering system.

If moisture is rising from the ground through a masonry foundation, a specially designed water proofing is required. Wood should not touch the ground anywhere on a building. Wall siding should begin at least six inches above the ground.

Once moisture problems have been

corrected, wood should be allowed to dry thoroughly after scraping and sanding. A "moisture meter", available at some local paint dealers, can be helpful in determining when wood has thoroughly dried. Once dry, the entire area should be sealed with a primer and finished with two finishing coats. More than adequate drying time should be allowed during periods of high temperature or humidity.

Mildew

Mildew or molds are fungi which thrive in nearly all environments. Mildew "feeds" on matter such as wood, paper, leather, and paint. Moisture content in the air is related directly to the growth capability of mildew. A surface with mildew growth must be treated effectively or mildew will reappear on paint which is applied over the fungi. Oil based paints can be particularly conducive to fungi growth.

Mildew can be killed and removed by scrubbing a surface with a commercial mildew wash or a solution of one part household bleach to three parts water. This should be followed by a detergent wash and fresh water rinse. If paint below the fungi is not damaged, repainting is unnecessary. If repainting is required, a mildewcide agent should be added to primer and paint to lessen chances of new mildew growth in the future.

MASONRY

Painted masonry was limited to elements above foundation level. Most commonly, this was brick. Structures built before 1850 were simple and constructed of soft brick. Clay was kiln-fired, baking the exterior surface only. The interior remained dried clay. Soft brick of this type was always painted to protect the fragile brick skin from damage which could expose the raw interior material.

More substantial houses used better quality brick which was solidly baked. It did not require painting, but many buildings of this type continued to be painted, emphasizing varied color combinations popular during the mid-nineteenth century.

Completely baked brick was available beginning in the late-nineteenth century. Much of this brick was unpainted since its natural surface was impervious to deterioration.

Peeling

Efflorescence is the most common cause of peeling on surfaces of mortar, brick, and poured or block concrete. Soluble salts are contained in these materials. When these salts are dissolved in water, they are carried to the material surface and remain after water has evaporated. These crystallized salts push the paint away from material surface which results in peeling. This phenomenon can be observed as white staining on unpainted brick surfaces.

Paint peeling can also be caused by water entering behind paint through cracks along sharp edges or deteriorated sections of brick.

Efflorescence must be removed before repainting. All flaking and chalking paint must be removed from the damaged area by bristle brushing or low pressure steam cleaning. A four percent (4%) solution of hydrofluoric acid or undiluted vinegar may be necessary to remove salt deposits.

Next, the surface should be rinsed with clear water to remove any deposits of dirt, powdered masonry, or chemical residue. Once the surface has dried, all cracks should be filled with masonry patching compound, latex concrete patch, or caulking compound. If the surface is very porous, an alkali-resistant primer or block filler should be applied before finishing coats. An exterior latex masonry paint should be used as it contains no oil base ingredients to react chemically with mortar elements.

METAL

Galvanized

Metal surface paint peeling is almost exclusively the result of improper surface preparation. Clean metal is the first and most important step in painting galvanized surfaces. All loose, flaking paint must be removed to expose bare metal. Then a conditioner or rust-proof galvanized metal primer should be used. Once the surface has been properly treated and primed, exterior enamels may be applied as finishing coats.

Iron Work

Fences, cresting, railings, and lawn furniture made of cast or wrought iron are all susceptible to paint failure due to subsurface rust. Cleaning is essential in securing a long lasting coating on iron work. All loose rust, scale, and dirt can be wire brushed from the surface. Commercially available compounds will aid in rust removal and neutralization. Strongly adhering paint should be lightly sanded to insure new finish adhesion. Once the metal is completely free from rust, powder, and dirt, the area should be primed immediately with a rust inhibiting primer. Finish coats can then be applied.

A variety of paint products and additives are available to treat individual problems such as those previously described. Paint dealers or manufacturers can be extremely helpful in these situations.

Some general rules do apply specifically to old materials. An oil additive used directly or mixed in oil-based paint or primer is an excellent lubricant for dried wood. Flexible caulk can be used to seal joints or fill cracks. The caulk should expand and contract with the material it is serving. Oil based primers are best for old, weathered surfaces and can be used with either latex or alkyd paints.

PROHIBITIONS

Colors and shades which have no historical precedent for the style of the structure to be painted is prohibited as is self-cleaning paint which chalks when wet. Separate body and trim colors shall be used whenever appropriate and possible. Painting previously unpainted brick surfaces is prohibited.

FOR MORE INFORMATION

Century of Color: Exterior Decoration for American Buildings, 1820-1920, Roger Moss, (Watkins Glen, New York: American Life Foundation), 1981.

"Practical Painting Pointers," X.I.M. Products, Inc., 1972.

Paint Problem Solver, National Decorative Products Association, St. Louis, MO. 1980.

Porter Paints: Products, Specifications, and Applications. Catalog No. 56, Porter Paint Co.

"How To Select and Use Latex Caulks," Rohm and Haas, Philadelphia, 1975.

"Mildew: Technical Division Scientific Circular #802," National Paint and Coating Association, Inc., Washington, D.C.

"Removing Exterior Paint," John F. Zirkle, The Old-House Journal Vol. VII, No. 6, June 1979.

"It's Not As Easy As It Looks," Patricia Poore, The Old-House Journal Vol. XI, No. 4, April 1981.

"Don't Blame The Paint," Clem Labine, The Old-House Journal Vol. IX, No. 4, April 1981.

"Historic Paint Research: Determining The Original Colors," Mathew J. Mosca, The Old-House Journal Vol. IX, No. 4, April 1981.

"Stripping Exterior Paint," Ronald A LabineSr., and Ronald A. Labine Jr., The Old-House Journal Vol. IX, No. 4, April 1981.

SHUTTERS

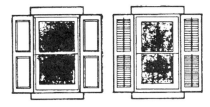

Exterior wood shutters served decorative and functional purposes on many styles of buildings constructed during the nineteenth century. Functionally, closed shutters with operable louvers permitted air flow and soft light to enter while shielding the house from intense sunlight and heat or rain. During winter months, closed shutters reduced heat loss and curbed drafts.

Visually, shutters were important style elements on many buildings built between 1830 and 1890, particularly on those of the Federal style. Locally, shutter usage varied among neighborhoods. Shutters provide a balancing effect between window openings and wall spaces; they minimize a large wall expanse and provide a more vertical appearance.

To determine if a building had shutters originally, the window casings can be checked for remaining hinge pins or notches in the wood where mountings could have been located.

A building possessing original, operable shutters is a rarity, and retention and rehabilitation of this element is important to preserve the character of the building. Some common problems with original shutters include missing or deteriorated parts and loose or non-functioning louvers and hinges. Frequently, shutter problems can be solved by stripping old paint from the piece. Shutters can be dismantled for repair or replacement of broken louvers, yoke pins, and/or rotted louver pegs.

Loose hinges cause shutters to sag and not close properly. Replacement with larger screws should eliminate this problem.

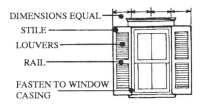

DIMENSIONS EQUAL
STILE
LOUVERS
RAIL
FASTEN TO WINDOW CASING

If the condition of original shutters is beyond repair, consider salvaging identically sized shutters from demolished structures or obtaining reproduction wood shutters with or without operable louvers.

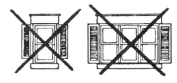

PROHIBITIONS

Vinyl or aluminum shutters are prohibited. Shutters must be of a size appropriate to cover the area of window sash they adjoin and must appear as though they could close. Shutters are to be either hung on hinges mounted to window casings or secured to wall with a one-inch spacer between the exterior wall and shutter.

FOR MORE INFORMATION

"Tips on Stripping Shutters," R. A. Labine, The Old-House Journal Vol. II, No. 9, September 1974.

"Restoring Shutters to Working Order," The Old-House Journal Vol. I, No. 2, November 1973.

AWNINGS

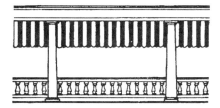

Canvas awnings for windows, doors, porches, and decks provide decorative protection from the elements. They offer a soft, flexible, textured component to a structure and are easily removable. Historically, awnings were used during summer months to reduce heat and fading damage to drapes, rugs, and furniture.

CANOPY

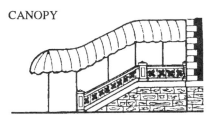

Awnings were available in a variety of shapes and colors. Over doorways, awnings frequently served as canopies, covering both the entry and steps. Window or door awnings could be umbrella-shaped, diagonal, or the more popular concave awning. Scalloped or straight edges with or without piping were common.

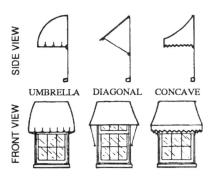

Storefront awnings extended out from the building to cover a portion of the sidewalk. Both commercial and residential awnings could be retracted; that is, rolled or folded back toward the building. Diagonal roll commercial awnings were used to enhance and protect open air uses such as fruit markets or similar vending.

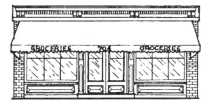

An awning is supported by steel posts which provide strength and shape. These posts are mounted to and project outward from a building and may also include a ground projecting support.

Canvas used in awnings is a durable and long lasting material when properly maintained. It is recommended that awnings be stored indoors during winter months. Occasionally, sections of the material can separate, thus requiring simple stitching. The material should be rubbed annually with a rejuvenating and sealing liquid designed to water proof canvas and keep it from becoming brittle.

Support framing, if damaged, requires replacement rather than repair. Individual sections are readily available from manufacturers.

Many companies custom manufacture an awning to a customer's specifications. Simple stripe patterns or solid colors are the most appropriate.

PROHIBITIONS

Soft, pliable canvas awnings cannot be duplicated with rigid metals such as aluminum and steel; therefore, only cloth awnings are permitted, and colors shall correspond with those appropriate to the building on which the awning is attached. However, contemporary design is permitted when in keeping with the architectural design standards.

Steel supports which are visible, i.e. ground projecting members, must be painted a dark color corresponding to that of the awning or the building on which the awning is located.

SUPPLEMENTAL
ELEMENTS

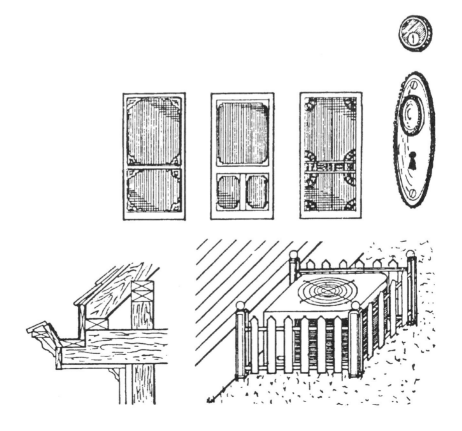

GUTTERS AND DOWNSPOUTS

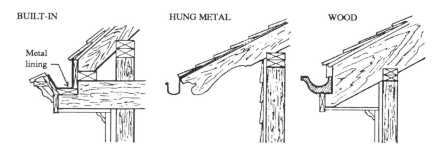

BUILT-IN   HUNG METAL   WOOD

Metal lining

Gutters and downspouts channel water runoff from a roof. Such systems collect water at the roof's edge and direct the flow to the ground below. Early gutter types included built-in or box, hung wood, and metal gutters. Many systems were custom made on site for each structure, particularly if the roofline was complex as in the case of curved sheet metal sections required for a Queen Anne tower.

Downspouts are located below roof valleys and at building corners. They are cylindrical sections of metal that direct water run-off away from a building's walls and foundation. The latter is accomplished by sections either extending underground connecting into a storm drain or placed on the ground facing away from the building.

Each type of gutter requires a different form of maintenance. A structure with a built-in gutter can suffer severe damage when it leaks into a box cornice. Careful monitoring of all seams in these metal lined gutters is required. Gutter liners made of tin, galvanized, or terne metal should be kept painted. Coating the lining with a roofing tar is not recommended due to the ability of water to penetrate the coating. Also, some coatings are acidic and can corrode metal.

Similarly, roof coatings should not be used on wood gutters. Problems arise as the tar hardens, while the wood below continues to expand and contract with the weather. This creates a gap between the coating and the wood, allowing water to enter, to become entrapped, and consequently to rot the wood gutter.

Best maintenance in this situation would be to chip out the old coating on a cold day when the coating is brittle. If this is not possible, liberal amounts of wood preservative should be forced into any cracks that could admit water. Wood gutters should be painted every three years on the inside, using two coats of asphalt roof paint thinned to a brushing consistency with one part thinner to four parts paint.

It is important that gutters do not become blocked by debris. Gutter and downspout seams should be checked and sealed, and sagging or loose gutters and downspouts should be securely mounted.

New aluminum gutter can be installed into existing cornice.

A drip strip guides water away from roof and into the gutter.

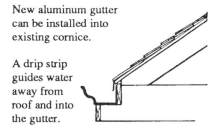

Aluminum gutters and downspouts may be used if original materials are missing or beyond repair. New gutters should be nailed directly to fascia or be incorporated into existing cornice or gutter systems. Gutters must slope one inch for every sixteen (16) feet of length to insure proper drainage. Splash blocks shall be placed at the outflow to channel water away from the house and minimize erosion around the foundation.

PROHIBITIONS

Wood, aluminum, and galvanized metal are appropriate gutter and downspout materials. All of these types shall be painted or, in the case of aluminum, may have a baked color finish. Gutters are to match building trim color while downspouts are to match trim or wall colors. Downspouts and gutters must not divide, destroy, or interfere with architectural details as this would adversely impact the design elements of the building. Downspouts must be placed at corners or along side of rear walls depending upon roof type, and gutters must include a drip strip which directs water into the gutter and away from the roof edge. Aluminum and metal gutters must be mounted to the fascia either directly or with the use of brackets. These procedures will contribute to the life of the gutter system as well as the roof structure.

FOR MORE INFORMATION

"Maintenance of Gutters," The Old-House Journal Vol. VII, No. 10, October 1979.

"Part II: Maintenance of Gutters," The Old-House Journal Vol. VII, No. 11, November 1979.

WEATHERPROOFING

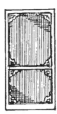 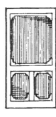 

Insulation and storm windows and doors are fairly recent innovations responding to the needs of an energy conscious society. The energy savings these products provide enable the economical retention of original decorative windows and doors and can be most effective in reducing energy losses in an old building.

Storm windows can be constructed of simple wood frames with glass inserts and installed over windows. Light-weight, flexible acrylic sheets with magnetic frames can be affixed to an interior window frame, thereby retaining a completely original facade. Wooden storm doors are available, also.

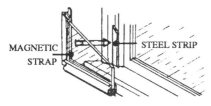

MAGNETIC STRAP   STEEL STRIP

Aluminum and vinyl-clad wood storm windows and aluminum storm doors can be manufactured to nearly any size and shape and can come in many color finishes. Doors with a plain horizontal lower panel or full view glass are quite

appropriate. Crossbuck colonial storm doors are prohibited as the style is not appropriate on pre-1950 buildings. Storm windows—if mounted on a frame house—must be placed on the blind stop part of the window. A brick building can have storm windows mounted on either the blind stop or the frame of the wndow. The storm window frame width shall be equal to or less than that of the original window.

Aluminum, wood, and vinyl-clad wood storm windows and doors shall be of a color compatible with the house trim color to minimize visual impact of the products. Raw (silver) aluminum or mill finish surfaces are prohibited as are storm doors designed primarily as security doors(for example, wrought iron).

APPROPRIATE
WOOD DOOR
DESIGN

Blown-in side wall insulation can be done through either the interior or exterior walls of a house. If the exterior walls are used, the caps placed in the walls after completion of the installation shall be wood. They must be installed flush with or counter sunk in the walls and painted to match the color of the surface into which they are installed. Plastic insulation plugs shall not be used.

PROHIBITIONS

Crossbuck colonial storm doors are prohibited. Storm window and door frames that are wider than the original openings are not permitted; they must fit existing openings. Raw (silver) aluminum or mill finish surfaces are prohibited

Plastic insulation plugs are not to be used.

FOR MORE INFORMATION

"Saving Energy in the Old House," Hartford Architecture Conservancy, Winter 1980.

"Screen Door Patterns" The Old-House Hournal Vol. VIII No. 7, July 1980.

UTILITIES

Electricity, plumbing, heating, ventilation, and air conditioning are modern living requirements which must be taken into account in any location. This includes other appurtenances such as television antennaes, satelite dishes, and cable wire. In the case of an historic building, which was most likely constructed before such systems existed, the locations should be as unobtrusive as possible.

Telephone, television, and electrical wires should be located at the rear of the property if run overhead. Ideally, they should be located underground. This is the case where a street pattern is established with underground utilities. Meters and boxes located on the exterior of a property must be located low on a side or rear building wall and shall be painted the color of that wall.

Television antennaes may be located on a roof at the rear of the house so as to be unnoticed. It is recommended that the antennae be located in the attic with the necessary wiring located at the rear of the roof.

Ventilation covers which are exposed on a building surface shall be painted to match that surface. Air conditioning condenser units are permitted at the rear of the property or on the sides if not

readily visible. If a prominent location is required, wood screening must surround the unit. Regardless of the location, however, air conditioning condenser units must be screened with landscaping. Window air conditioners are permitted since they are temporary and are classified as personal property. However, in no instance can windows be permanently reconfigured to accommodate the units nor can openings be cut into building walls for the placement of air conditioning units.

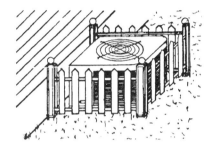

Solar panels can be used but must be located in such a way that they will have minimal impact on the streetscape.

PROHIBITIONS

Again, in order to minimize their impact, utilities of any type may not be located on the front facade or roof face or the front half of either side of any building.

HOME SECURITY

Home security is a realistic considera-tion which can be accomplished quite successfully with minimal impact to a building. Deadbolt locks, safety glass, and electronic alarm systems are virtually unnoticeable, yet can provide a considerable degree of protection.

Security can be upgraded by the addition of lighting, particularly at locations where landscaping is espe-cially heavy. Also, decorative elements, such as shutters, can be closed and locked from the inside, providing security and aesthetic appropriateness simultaneously.

Basement windows may be installed with glass blocks(no vents) as long as they fit the existing opening, have a 2" recess, and are located on non-streetside elevations.

Ironically, there is nothing more damaging to a business district than an appearance of heavy security or forti-fication. The presence of bars along windows or roll-down security gates across street level windows shows fear on the part of the property owners and implies that others should also be fearful. This discourages people from patronizing the stores in the neighbor-hood.

PROHIBITIONS

In addition, iron bars serve as a dan-gerous fire trap, hampering a quick escape by a building's occupants. They eliminate the ability of firefighters to gain entry, rescue victims, and stop a fire from spreading to adjacent proper-ties. Because such a window and door treatment is a safety hazard, is not his-torically accurate, and does not contri-bute aesthetically to an historic struc-ture, iron bars and wrought iron security doors are prohibited.

On commercial building storefronts, roll-down security gates are permitted if mounted on the inside; if mounted on the outside, they must be recessed and have a hood covering over the roll. In all instances, the gates are to be up during normal business hours and to be in a color compatible with the buiding. Raw aluminum, silver, or mill finishes are prohibited.

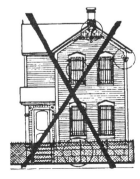

BUILDING IDENTIFICATION

front facade of the particular building or toward the street frontage of a vacant lot.

PROHIBITIONS

Both printed and written wording for address numerals, raw aluminum, and wood for numerals or markers are not permitted as they are inappropriate in design and material.

Historical markers and address numerals are the most common forms of building identification. Street addresses are used by police and fire departments, postmen, visitors, and neighbors to locate and refer to a particular building or parcel of land. Historical markers denote significant information connected with a property and often include the original owner or builder or an important event which occurred on the site.

717 81 11
419 522 900
214 38 169 651
24

Address numerals must be between three and eight inches in height and may be made of iron, wood, brass, aluminum, or can be stencilled on window glass or awnings. Their color should complement that of the building on which they are located.

All means of identification should face the public street. Additionally, address numerals should be on garages accessed from alleys for public safety reasons. Plaques and markers should be on the

NEW
CONSTRUCTION

PRIMARY STRUCTURES

Streetscape rhythm was an extremely important feature of an historical urban setting. It consisted of a pattern of building facades with similar street setbacks and spacing between each building. Commonality of shape, size, height, and roofline created an order which was readily identifiable.

Individual neighborhoods could be recognized by the building patterns and street grid systems prevalent in the area. Perpendicular gridding with long, narrow lots was the common urban development pattern. The smaller of the lot dimensions denoted the street frontage since frontage constituted a great expense.

NEW BUILDING SHOULD BORROW ELEMENTS FROM BLOCK FACE TO MAINTAIN UNITY

Buildings conformed to the proportions of the lot until a property owner's increased economic status warranted greater individuality of design and location. Large homes with spacious lawns did not become prevalent until an area's residents could afford to exhibit their material wealth.

The pattern of houses on a street is significant as is the design and construction of the individual houses. A building's relationship to its neighbors reflects part of its own identity. Compatible characteristics begin with building proportion and shape and then proceed to the location and size of window and door openings and porches. Finally, rhythm is completed by the use of compatible materials.

However, streetscape rhythm is interrupted when a building is demolished. A subsequent structure of a different size, shape, and height destroys blockface unity. A similar case exists when window and door openings are altered.

New construction which maintains the proportions of wall height and length, window and door opening sizes, and roof height and slope is a valuable complement to a streetscape. Adjacent structures provide the standards for the new structure to follow. Detailing on a new primary structure should be sympathetic in design, scale, proportion, and materials to the body of the building, but should not replicate that of the historic architecture of the block.

regard to contemporary techniques and materials and, more importantly, who understands the delicate relationship between historic and contemporary architecture, is necessary. A trained professional can coordinate all of the steps or phases required to complete the construction satisfactorily.

PROHIBITIONS

New construction must maintain streetscape rhythm and structural proportions of the surrounding buildings. Detailing shall be compatible with the design and shall be included on the building. Refer to appropriate sections for specific design requirements of the many different elements which comprise a new building.

CONSTRUCT A SYMPATHETIC INFILL STRUCTURE

Construction of a new primary structure is a complex process which requires a thorough knowledge of building techniques and local regulatory codes. A new building in an existing neighborhood, particularly one composed of historic architecture, requires considerable sensitivity and awareness of design features.

Retaining the services of a design professional who is competent with

BUILDING ADDITIONS

Living space requirements have always varied between occupants. Often, the existing building could not fulfill the living space needs of its occupants and required expansion. Many buildings have experienced several additions throughout their lifetimes. Early additions were attached kitchens and bathrooms which were built as indoor plumbing and gas or electricity became available. As a family expanded in size or wealth, bedrooms and sunrooms were also added.

Sometimes, these additions did not receive workmanship comparable to that exercised on the original building. Consequently, the additions may not be structurally sound, and removal is necessary. The addition can be rebuilt

POINTERS FOR A SYMPATHETIC ADDITION

EXISTING HOUSE | NEW ADDITION

- SHINGLES SAME AS EXISTING
- SIDING TO MATCH ORIGINAL MATERIAL AND DESIGN
- UNNEEDED WINDOW OPENING SHUTTERED
- NEW WINDOW OPENINGS DUPLICATE EXISTING RHYTHM, SIZE, AND TRIM

properly with materials, techniques, and design sympathetic to the original building and within existing building and fire codes.

Similarly, a house can be expanded to provide living space not previously existing. Construction materials should be compatible with the original building's materials. Brick, stone, and rough-faced block are appropriate foundation materials; wood, hardboard, brick, and stone are acceptable wall materials. In both of these cases, the original building's fabric dictates the materials to be used for the addition so that it will match or complement the original building. Window and door openings are to be of similar proporations and placement as those on the original building. Roof design and materials should also directly relate to that of the original building.

UNACCEPTABLE ADDITION TO REAR OF A BUILDING

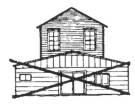

Materials which are not permitted for building additions are identical to those prohibited for original or new construction. Reference can be made to specific sections of the manual for detailed listings. For the most part, no additions shall be made to the front of a building.

STRUCTURAL PROPORTION

Structural proportion, or scale, refers to the way a building fits into its surroundings. Most neighborhoods that were constructed before the advent of the automobile were oriented to the pedestrian since most people walked as their primary mode of transportation. In neighborhood business districts, large structures were uncommon as there were few large businesses to be housed.

When new buildings were constructed in business districts, they had to be oriented to the pedestrian so that the businesses operating in them could compete effectively with those in nearby buildings. Consequently, the overall effect was that of a group of buildings that belonged together as a single unit. It was easy to establish the identity and character of a business district, and this in turn helped business in the area.

Whether the location is in the residential or business section of the district, new construction or additions to existing structures should maintain the structural proportions and scale of the existing neighborhood. This means conforming to the setbacks already established on the blockface and building to the approximate height of neighboring buildings. Larger structures can be fit into the streetscape by breaking the facade into smaller bays that are similar in size to the smaller structures nearby. The overall effect should be of a building that looks as if it belongs in the setting in which is has been placed.

New construction should not, however, attempt to produce an exact replica of a past historical style. Such an attempt often looks artificial and detracts from the surrounding district. Building materials and colors should be compatible with nearby structures as well as the scale of the building.

PROHIBITIONS

Materials which are not permitted for building additions are identical to those prohibited for original or new construct-

ion. Refer to specific sections of the manual for detailed listings. For the most part, no additions shall be made to the front of a structure.

ACCESSORY STRUCTURES

Household functions which were not accomplished within a house usually were accommodated in a secondary building, such as a smokehouse, springhouse, carriage house, garage, and, to a lesser extent, gazebo or greenhouse. These secondary buildings were smaller and usually simpler in design than was the primary building but reflected the same design characteristics.

These accessory buildings are frequently original to the site or have some historical basis. Sensitive adaptations, particularly to carriage houses or garages, can provide modern, functional space while retaining the historic character of the building and enhancing the entire property.

Carriage houses and garages were and continue to be the most commonly desired outbuildings. Historically, a

carriage house was a two-story building located to the rear of a property which served as a shelter initially for buggies and later for automobiles. Space was provided for garden tools, lawnmowers, and other implements with an ample area on the second floor for storage.

Garages were built in the early twentieth century specifically for automobiles. They were one-story in height and did not feature the floor area available in a carriage house. A separate entry was provided for each vehicular section with one and two bays being the most frequently constructed. Vehicular doors for garages or carriage barns may be flush or feature retangular panels and may include windows.

DESIGN FOR NEW GARAGE & GREENHOUSE

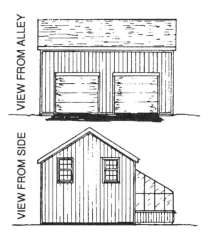

VIEW FROM ALLEY

VIEW FROM SIDE

Gazebos and greenhouses became fashionable during the late nineteenth century accompanying the development of a wide variety of plant materials. A gazebo is a small open sided or screened structure used decoratively as part of a landscape plan. Greenhouses were either freestanding or attached to a building and used the sun's energy passing through sections of glass to grow plants.

All accessory buildings should be designed to complement the primary building on the site. Detailing may be simpler on the accessory building. Standards for items such as roofs, doors, windows, and wall materials are the same as those for primary buildings and are listed in the section addressing the specific item.

APPROPRIATE
VEHICULAR
DOOR DESIGNS

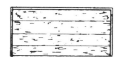

ROUGH SAWN FLUSH DOOR

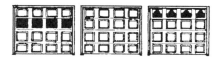

PANELLED DOORS (windows acceptable)

Vehicular doors for garages or carriage barns may be flush or feature rectangular panels. They may include windows.

PROHIBITIONS

Materials which are not permitted for accessory structures are identical to those prohibited for original or new construction. Reference can be made to specific sections of the manual for detailed listings.

LANDSCAPING

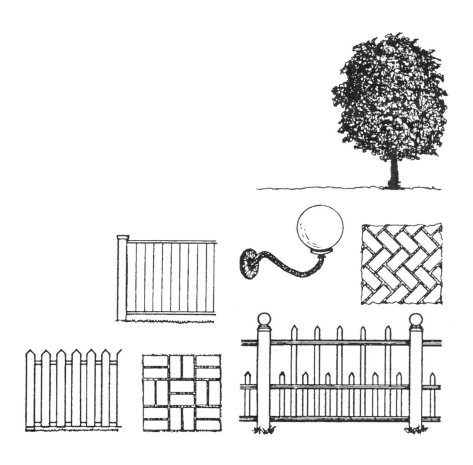

LAWNS AND GARDENS

Historically, a yard was the portion of the property where chores were performed or animals were kept. Vegetable gardens and fruit trees were located in the yard as were barns, sheds, and other outbuildings.

A garden included plantings and a lawn or grass area which served primarily a decorative purpose. This area featured fountains, urns, statues, and gazebos framed by a colorful variety of plants and shrubs.

Adaptation of this rural setting to an urban neighborhood with buildings in close proximity eliminated most of the

need for the yard area and scaled down the garden space. The site continued to be organized according to function, with an additional requirement of privacy. Consequently, public, private, and utility areas occupied neighborhood landscapes.

The specific components of these landscape areas corresponded to the building style dominating the site. Symmetry and regularity found in early and mid-nineteenth century Greek Revival and Italianate styled buildings required formal, stately gardens featuring one or two brilliantly colored plants. These included fuchsia, red

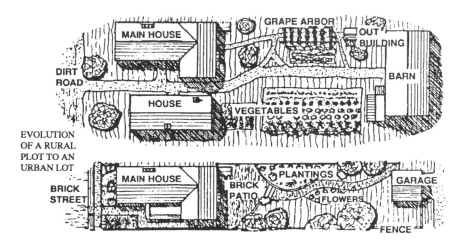

geranium, mock-orange, lilac, lobelia, and salvia.

The Gothic style originated in a secluded, woodsy atmosphere which characterized the transplant of the style and its landscape to urban areas. Thick growths of trees providing heavy shade and rusticity surrounded the building. During this time, vines such as honeysuckle were twined on wires around porches, up downspouts, and around bay windows. This enhanced the wild, natural setting.

The late nineteenth century witnessed the heyday of architectural imagination. Queen Anne styled buildings, thriving on their irregularity of design and attention to detail, demanded a companion setting of considerable intricacy. Geometric flowerbeds—best appreciated from upper-story windows—were ablaze with colorful flowers and shrubs. American elms, European beeches, and silver maples encircled many a Queen Anne's towers and turrets. Further ornamentation was provided by the use of statuary, arbors, and gazebos.

Plants popularized during the mid- and late nineteenth century include Japanese yew, viburnum, weigelia, Japanese barberry, quince, hydrangea, and Boston ivy. Also, flowers such as peraniums, coleus, nasturtiums, alyssums, and zinnias were developed.

The turn of the twentieth century experienced a freedom in building styles and a relaxed landscape plan. Colonial Revivals and Foursquares depended upon perennials planted in gently curving groupings framing the focal point of the landscape—the lawn. A large expanse of manicured grass became practical during this time

because of the invention of the lawnmower. Foundation plantings were also used.

Prairie style houses utilized willow, cottonwood, and elm trees to enhance their horizontal, flowing designs. Trees assumed a more prominent role in a landscape plan while annuals received minimal consideration. Also planting boxes became an integral part of the structure and emphasized the horizontal lines of the structure.

New landscaping in keeping with the size, scale, and design of the primary structure on the property is welcomed. In the case of a vacant lot or parking areas, concentrations of canopy trees are effective in increasing the vertical appearance of the lot.

Plants used in the nineteenth and early twentieth centuries, such as those mentioned earlier in this section, are recommended. Ornamentation—statuary, foundations, etc.—is welcomed, also. However, trees other than ornamental are not permitted to be planted around the foundation of a structure due to potential conflicts between a tree's root system and the foundation. Also, ivy growing on a foundation or wall can deteriorate mortar or paint and therefore is prohibited.

Rough or cut limestone—in pieces or slabs—and paving brick are ideal walk materials, unlike dirt, wood, or asphalt which are not appropriate to urban settings. Paving brick should be laid in a herring bone, basketweave, or running bond pattern. Street pavers—larger and heavier than paving brick—and concrete sections are appropriate as well. Rear yard walks may use limestone or gravel chips.

BRICK PAVING PATTERNS

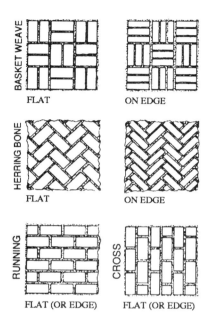

growing on a foundation or wall can deteriorate mortar or paint and therefore is prohibited.

Dirt, wood, or asphalt walkways are prohibited.

Vegetable gardens are recommended to be located in the rear yard.

FOR MORE INFORMATION

Hartford Architecture Conservancy, "Landscaping the Old House," Spring 1979.

Goode, Stacy, Jackson, "Building an Old Fashioned Garden," The Old-House Journal, February 1978.

Jeanloz, Donna, "Victorian Landscaping," The Old-House Journal, April 1977.

Gerhardt, Tom. "Victorian Cast Iron Fountains and Urns," The Old-House Journal, June and July 1977.

Pilling, Ron, "Brick Walks," The Old-House Journal , July 1980.

Driveway or parking pad standards are the same as those for walks but include asphalt.

Decks are permitted when they are constructed of wood with beveled rails and inset spindles. Designs must be appropriate and compatible with the main structure and design elements already existing. Any new design elements (i.e. lattice) must conform with the stipulations covered in this manual.

PROHIBITIONS

Trees, other than ornamental, are not permitted to be planted around the foundation of a structure due to the pontential conflicts between a tree's root system and the foundation. Also, ivy

FENCES & GATES

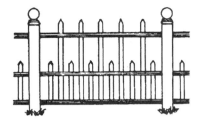

Fences and gates originally were physical barriers or property dividers. Initially, they served functional purposes only and were constructed of simple materials. Since they marked boundary lines which could be changed, they were designed to be easily dismantled.

Beginning in the eighteenth century, fences and gates served as decorative elements enhancing individual buildings. They were incorporated into the design scheme for the site and reflected the size and style of the adjacent building. Fences and gates, particularly wrought and cast iron, provided an opportunity for the exhibition of fine craftsmanship in a highly visible location. Rows of glossy black iron provided visual interest along a streetscape.

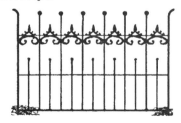

Rear yard fences provided private space to enjoy the outdoors. Frequently, they ranged from four to six feet in height and were constructed of wood. Again, their designs complemented the primary building on the site; however, they were most often simple in style compared to the more public front yard fence.

Wood fences were used around both front and rear yards with the same stylistic standards applicable to iron. Simple picket fences popular during early years of development matured into the intricate and flamboyant designs of the Victorian era.

In the late nineteenth century and early twentieth century with the birth of suburbs, large and expansive front lawns devoid of fences became the standard. Many properties included deed restrictions to prevent front yard fences and to maintain the harmony of the streetscape.

Like other elements exposed to the weather, both cast and wrought iron will rust. Ordinarily, this will occur along joints where pieces have been welded or at weak spots where damage has occurred. Repair can be made by rewelding or by bolting pieces together followed by sanding and painting with a metal primer and paint.

BUILDING A PICKET FENCE

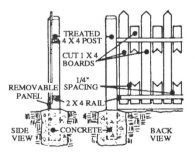

Wood fences can have pieces or sections replaced or repaired. If the area is small, grafting a new piece to an existing member is satisfactory. Paint each piece prior to attachment and use aluminum or galvanized nails to avoid rusting. Horizontal supports must be on the owner's side for aesthetic and security reasons.

Nearly any design can be executed in wood or iron but, due to varying complexity, can be expensive. Simple designs are stocked by distributors and are readily available. Antique iron fencing can be obtained through antique dealers or from demolition contractors.

APPROPRIATE
FENCE
PRODUCTS

ORNAMENTAL WIRE*

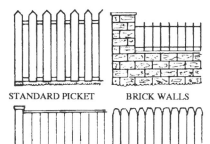

STANDARD PICKET   BRICK WALLS

STRAIGHT BOARD   FRENCH GOTHIC

*For side and rear yards only

Fences which are in keeping with the design and period of the building or site which they border make an important contribution to the environment of that historic property. Wood and iron fences and brick and stone walls help define and complement the scale of surrounding buildings.

PROHIBITIONS
Specifically prohibited are chain link, expanded mesh, and horse wire metal fencing. These fence types were used historically in industrial or rural areas

for functional reasons and are inappropriate in urban historic neighborhoods. Also not permitted are split rail and basketweave wood fences. Both are out of character with urban nineteenth and twentieth century streetscapes and are appropriate for primitive, rural, or suburban settings.

Select a fence and gate type which compliments the site on which it is to be located. Notice the size, style, and materials of any structure on the property when selecting a fence and gate type, and erect one which will unify the whole rather than one which detracts from the character of the property and streetscape.

PROHIBITED
FENCING

CHAIN LINK

BARBED WIRE   HORSE WIRE

SPLIT RAIL   BASKETWEAVE

FOR MORE INFORMATION

Herman, Frederick, AIA, "Fences, Part I, II, III," The Old-House Journal Vol. VII, Nos. 2,3,4. February, March, April 1979.

LIGHTING

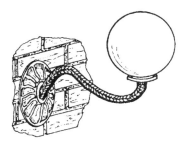

Lighting which is not of a decorative nature appropriate to the design of the primary structure and its site is not permitted; neither are plain aluminum pole lamps and large flood lights as they are inappropriate.

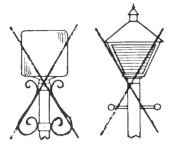

Outdoor lighting for a building or its grounds is encouraged. Decorative fixtures mounted on building facades or in a porch area enhance a building's style in addition to being functional. This lighting should reflect the design of the building, if highly visible.

FLOOD LIGHTS SHOULD BE LOCATED UNDER EAVES

Flood lighting is permitted; however, the location of the fixture should not detract from the building to which the fixture is attached. For example, a wide eave would conceal a flood lamp and provide excellent light to the surrounding grounds.

Yard lighting can be in the form of iron, wood, or decorative aluminum based pole lamps or small decorative walk and garden lights. The size of the yard, particularly the prominent front facade, constitutes the major factor in selecting outdoor lighting.

NON-RESIDENTIAL BUILDINGS

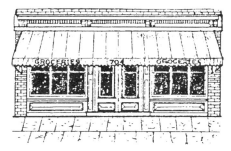

COMMERCIAL

The commercial areas that are located in several of the historic districts serve as "front doors" to the districts since they are situated along important thoroughfares. Built before the widespread ownership of automobiles, these commercial areas were characterized by small shops oriented toward pedestrians and the streetcar trade.

The rise in automobile usage coincided with and contributed to the decline of many inner city commercial districts which were hard pressed to compete with the new suburban strip centers. Typical solutions to this dilemma included the razing of buildings for more parking, the "modernization" of storefronts, and the installation of large, garish signs to attract attention.

These improvements failed to provide a cure for the decline, however. They may even have been detrimental because the unique character of the historic commercial districts was compromised in order to compete with newer shopping centers which had advantages such as better parking and a more affluent customer base that older areas could not provide.

However, these competitive disadvantages can be partially overcome by playing on the districts' unique historic and architectural character. To bring out this character, though, means changing the standard approach to commercial building alterations. It means removing inappropriate attempts at modernization and restoring much of the original buildings' hidden details. Improving the appearance of businesses gives a favorable impression to outsiders, some of whom may become interested in conducting business or even living nearby. This, in turn, would benefit existing businesses by improving sales and triggering further cycles of improvement.

The street facade is the most recognizable portion of most commercial buildings. Almost everything one needs to know about what occupies the building can be found by looking at the facade. This is where the main entrance and storefronts are usually found as well as signage and other indications of life.

The street facade is also where most of the decorative detailing can be found. This detailing serves the function of making the building look less ordinary, thereby attracting both tenants and customers. However minor it may seem in individual cases, the sum total of this detailing gives the block a comfortable feel that separates it from plainer areas that may exist nearby. Such a unique identity is important to the health of the commercial district, hence, the importance of maintaining these features.

The information presented in this section describes construction elements of commercical, institutional, and industrial buildings. Only elements which vary from those for residential buildings are addressed in this section. Standards which pertain to architectural elements common to all building types

are covered in individual sections, i.e. *Shutters, Windows,* and so on.

STOREFRONTS

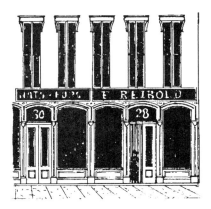

In the 1840's, business buildings acquired a character of their own with the innovation of the storefront. This first-story treatment featured large display windows and a formal entry while upper stories retained residential characteristics.

The shop windows were flanked by vertical supports, or pilasters. Constructed of wood, stone, or cast iron, these pilasters—capped by a horizontal support or cornice—provided an inviting frame for the displayed articles. The business entry was frequently recessed to avoid competition with the display area.

Throughout the late nineteenth century, storefronts underwent several changes. Glass expanses became larger and exhibited fewer divisions. Art glass was sometimes used for design detail and as a means of providing visual interest.

Horizontal panels(knee walls), beginning at ground level and rising a couple of feet, served as the practical conclusion to the storefront display area. Constructed of wood or iron, they were immune to breakage and weather damage and provided the visual fourth side of the glass frame.

Canvas awnings were most extensively used over commercial storefronts. Serving as an advertising medium with signs, they provided shelter for shoppers and extended the display surface; merchandise could be set under the awnings to be viewed by passersby and simultaneously could be protected from summer sun and rain.

Awnings may extend the length of the storefront facade, or they may cover only a portion of that facade such as the display windows or the entry. Also, separate awnings may be used across the facade with breaks at the structural supports.

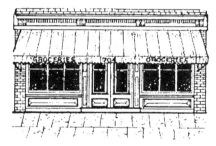

The early twentieth century witnessed the construction of one-story flat-roofed commerical buildings which relied on large expanses of clear-vision glass for openness. Detailing was minimal, frequently limited to decorative brick or stonework incorporated into the structural configuration of the building.

Repairs to storefronts frequently consist of replacing glass, guidelines for which can be found in the *Windows* section. Replacement of damaged horizontal panels can be accomplished by removal

of the window section and replacement in-kind of the deteriorated material. Panels were usually one inch (1") thick boards with molding or trim added to the facing. In cases where storefront treatment was cast iron, iron covered the wood panels. This iron can be replicated commercially, if damaged.

Likewise, a damaged pilaster can be duplicated if necessary as most were simple in design. If the pilaster is of limestone and is severely damaged, the weight it supports can be transfered with a jack while the pilaster is replaced. A new pilaster can be fashioned from wood in the design of the original stone pilaster.

Cast iron storefronts consisted of non-structural metal covering unadorned wood to provide great detail to the surface. The iron was always painted, often to simulate limestone—light gray/white—or sandstone—dark red/brown. Paint also served to protect the surface from rust.

Sensitive storefront alterations to accommodate a building's particular function are appropriate. Closed interior shutters or blinds and pulled shades guarantee privacy. Exterior shutters affixed to the window openings and presenting an appearance of closed shutters can be used when security is warranted; however, a first alternative would be to use tempered or safety glass.

PROHIBITIONS

Attempts at "modernization" such as the installment of metal wall panels and the reduction or elimination of window space distracts from the historic function of a building and has a deadening effect on a street that is detrimental to the continuing prosperity of nearby businesses. Such "improvements" either must not be undertaken or should be reversed by their removal. Usually, such a removal will reveal that the original, hidden facade is surprisingly intact and requires only minor repairs to bring it back to its former state.

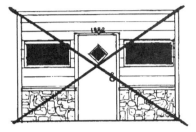

Treatments which would alter the proportion and scale of the storefront by the removal of the windows, pilasters, and/or horizontal panels shall not be used. Storefront treatments utilizing few visible supports and large uninterrupted expanses of glass, metal, vinyl, or wood are not appropriate.

Aluminum, steel, and vinyl awnings are prohibited; only canvas awnings are permitted. See *Awnings* section for additional related information.

UPPER FACADES

The portions of commercial buildings located above the first story or street frontage usually emulated residential buildings of the same era. Early and mid-nineteenth century buildings featured plain, symmetrical facades with multi-paned, elongated, double hung windows flanked by operable shutters. When ornamentation became fashionable, upper facades incorporated decorative window hoods and heavy, bracketed and paneled cornices.

The asymmetry of the Queen Anne style was attempted to a small degree on commercial buildings through the incorporation of towers, turrets, and dormers on upper facades.

A few years later, flamboyant detailing executed in terra cotta added interest to commercial buildings which included large windows throughout the building as a prominent design element. The terra cotta provided a material which permitted great depth of detail to be exhibited and allowed the execution of minute elements to be made effectively.

Damage to upper facades (regardless of the material), including the cornice, is comparable to that found on residential buildings, and repairs can be accomplished similarly, also. Reference can be made to the appropriate sections.

PROHIBITIONS

Removal or alteration of window and door openings, detailing, and materials on a prominent facade is prohibited as it has a direct and strong impact on the design, massing, and scale of the building itself as well as how it relates to those buildings surrounding it. Closed shutters can be used in a window opening where glass is not desired so as to maintain the balance of the building. Covering upper facades with metal, vinyl, wood, and glass is not permitted. Other concerns can be found under individual building element sections, i.e. *Windows, Walls*.

FOR MORE INFORMATION

"Old Storefronts, 1870-1920," Mara Glebloom, The Old-House Journal Vol. VI No. 7, March 1978.

Richmond Architectural Renovation, The Downtown Development Office, Richmond, Virginia.

Combination Atlas Map of Montgomery County, Ohio, L. H. Everts, 1875.

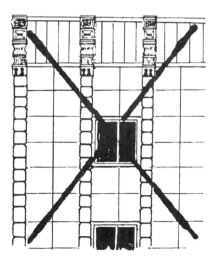

INSTITUTIONAL

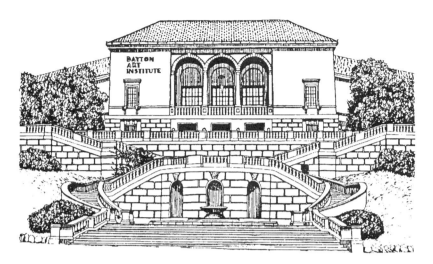

Institutional buildings are primarily churches and schools. The latter were built in styles and with detailing similar to residences constructed during the same era—but on a grander scale. Churches were frequently built in the commanding Gothic or Romanesque styles. Both churches and schools were executed almost exclusively in masonry—frequently brick with stone trim.

Standards for appropriate repairs and alterations to institutional structures correspond to those specified in individual sections of this manual.

PROHIBITIONS

As in previously discussed sections, the removal or alteration of window and door openings, detailing, and materials on a prominent facade is not permitted. Additional prohibitions can be found under individual building element sections, i.e. *Windows, Doors.*

INDUSTRIAL

Industrial structures were usually large, multi-story buildings devoid of a public entryway. They had few, if any, architectural details. Industrial buildings were often constructed of masonry and were symmetrical in design.

Repairs and alterations to industrial buildings shall correspond to those appropriate for individual elements of residential buildings as described in this manual. Some alterations may incorporate standards which would be appropriate for accessory structures. An example would be a loading bay requiring a vehicular entry door which would correspond to a residential garage door.

PROHIBITIONS

Again, as previously discussed, removal or alteration of window and door openings, detailing, and materials on a prominent facade is not permitted. Additional prohibitions can be found under individual building element sections, i.e. *Windows, Doors.*

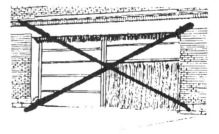

SIGNAGE

Signs serve the dual purpose of identifying a business and advertising the product or services sold by a particular establishment. They are often the most noticeable elements of a commercial street scene. Historically, business signs were located on the horizontal member over the storefront or hung on iron brackets at the same level and extending over the public sidewalk. Also, signs were painted directly upon a building, particularly for a corner location on the facade which did not feature the storefront. Temporary signs advertising a particular product were made of wood or metal and placed immediately in front of the business on the public sidewalk.

When there is a large concentration of businesses, there is sometimes a tendency to construct ever larger signs in order to remain noticeable. The result is a mish-mash of signs that are difficult to distinguish, dangerous for motorists,

and destructive to the historic character of the area. Paradoxically, such an approach, designed to promote business at a particular establishment, is a detriment to healthy business in the whole district.

It is important, then, to keep signage simple and unobtrusive. The sign should be small and contain only the most basic information. The name of the establishment and its main line of business should suffice, i.e. "Smith's Drugstore."

Contemporary signage should follow the historical pattern. A sign is a design element and should complement the building style and proportion on which it is located. Confusion reigns when signs are mounted in a seemingly random manner on a building. Signs should be limited to the lintel, windows, and the awnings. Projecting signs are permitted only over the main entrance to the store. A large sign should be mounted in front of the storefront cornice while small signs should be located over entryways and hung on iron brackets or other decorative supports. Small temporary signs are permitted when in keeping with the remainder of the signage.

Lettering is also an important aspect of coherent signage. Signs are easier to read if the business owner keeps to one style of lettering rather than an assortment of styles which may reduce readability. Lettering can generally be described as either *serif* or *sans serif* and should be entirely one or the other.

Symbols, such as barber's pole or a mortar and pestle for a pharmacy, are also appropriate forms of signage; however, their size should be commensurate with the scale of the building. The amount of space devoted to symbols will be subtracted from the total allowed for signs.

Identification signs in scale with the building on which they are located are permitted; however, they shall not exceed 100 square feet of total sign area. Sign scale shall be determined by the mathematical ratio of the height and width of the building on which the sign is to be located or that portion thereof. Projecting identification signs may not exceed 32 square feet, or 16 square feet per face. Two or less signs per business use are permitted.

Ground projecting signs are permitted only at parking lots, where the building setback is greater than that established on the street, or in instances where the building set back is consistantly deep. Ground projecting signs may also be permitted in cases of multi-tenant commercial usage in lieu of numerous wall mounted signs. Concealed, exterior lighting is recommended. Traffic control and historic district identification signs are permitted.

APPROPRIATE SIGNAGE

PROHIBITIONS

Certain types of signs that have traditionally been used on highway oriented thoroughfares are clearly inappropriate to a historic district given

the pedestrian oriented nature of the street. These include moving and flashing signs, plastic signs, billboards, portable signs, advertising signs, and poster panel/billboard signs. Signs extending above the wall of any structure to which they are attached are prohibited.

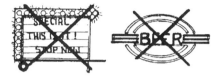

PUBLIC
IMPROVEMENTS

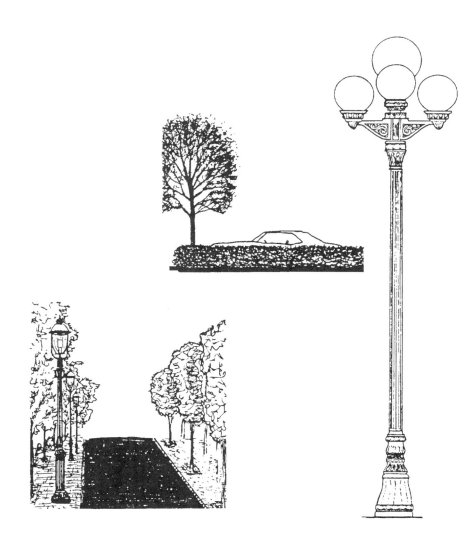

PARKS

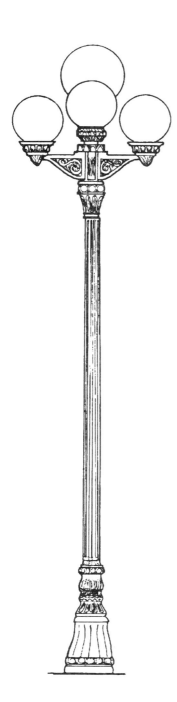

A well-planned neighborhood park can well serve the leisure needs of area residents and be aesthetically pleasing. Green space is an important feature in any area, but to built urban neighborhoods, this space may provide the only outdoor recreation area for nearby residents.

Historically, parks functioned similarly to the way they do today. Areas were established for active and passive recreation. Play equipment was available as were benches and walkways. Many times, the park served as a meeting area and featured a bandshell or gazebo for picnics and concerts.

Brick, stone, wood, and iron are effective materials to enhance a park set in an historic area. Plants from an earlier era are appropriate, also. The *Landscaping—Lawns and Gardens—* section describes historic plant material. Color should be provided by the plantings with other elements, such as benches or play equipment, taking a subdued, secondary role.

Lighting is important, also, and should be designed and scaled to pedestrians. It should be decorative and suit the other materials used in the park.

STREETS, ALLEYS, AND WALKS

Early in the twentieth century, brick replaced earlier road materials, such as dirt and gravel. Street bricks were solidly fired clay which were larger and heavier than building bricks. They were laid in a running bond pattern.

Curbs were usually of limestone, often cut in sections of several feet in length and, less frequently, rough but uniformly sized pieces of rough quarried stone.

Sidewalks were also of limestone or sandstone, laid in flat sheets approximately six feet square. These walks did very little settling once in place due to their weight. Also, because of the denseness of the stone, vegetation seldom found its way to the surface.

Retention of early thoroughfare materials is desirable since those materials add historical significance to an area. Furthermore, brick and stone were primary nineteenth century construction materials and therefore, harmonize with the extant historic building fabric.

Another prevalent thoroughfare feature was trees. The area between the sidewalk and street is the tree lawn where grass, flowers, and shrubs were frequently present. However, the most common feature was large, leaf bearing trees. They served as a soft physical barrier between buildings and roadways.

Also in the tree lawn were street lights, hitching posts, and carriage steps. These items are currently rare, but are important in retaining the character of a neighborhood.

Settling may occur on a walk or a street, particularly if the latter handles heavy traffic or serves as a truck route. The simplest means of repair for a street is to pry up the bricks which are damaged or settled, place some gravel in the space, turn over the bricks, and replace them. A damaged limestone or sandstone walk requires raising the sunken portion and reinforcing the ground below the walk section. Prying up the section or digging around it and pouring gravel or concrete into the space should prohibit further settling.

Brick is readily available from building material suppliers or salvage dealers. Limestone is much scarcer and, therefore, is difficult to obtain. Brick can be used in place of limestone for sidewalks. If a pattern, such as herringbone, has been established on a block, it should be continued.

PROHIBITIONS

Asphalt sidewalks and tree lawns are not permitted; neither are painted sidewalks, streets, or alleys.

PARKING LOTS

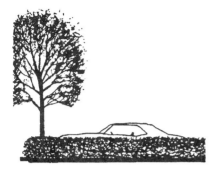

Parking facilities are not original features of most historic areas. Many times, they are created following the demolition of buildings, all too often on the interior of a block. Scale as well as architectural fabric is destroyed in the process.

In order to reunify a blockface which has been affected by demolition, height must be re-established where the building was removed. A fence or wall at the setback line accomplishes this. Vegetation can be successful, also, but is a more temporary solution; if trees or shrubs are damaged or die, the tendency may be not to replace them. A fence or wall in conjunction with landscaping is a more satisfactory solution.

If a parking lot is located in front of or to the side of a building, landscaping within the lot is required in order to visually minimize the "sea of asphalt" appearance. Again, height is important and can be established with the use of caliper trees.

Lighting should be decorative and should be compatible with the primary era of the blockface or historic districts.

GLOSSARY

WALLS AND FOUNDATIONS

BRICK - KILN-FIRED CLAY MOLDED INTO A MASONRY UNIT

Half-Brick - Brick split lengthwise; used for ornamentation

Hard Brick - Brick fired quickly, at high temperatures, baking the interior as well as the exterior surface; twentieth century

Pressed Brick - Brick molded into a compact smooth face by mechanical pressure; after 1890

Soft Brick - Brick fired at a temperature, baking the exterior surface but leaving the interior soft

BRICK BOND - PATTERN IN WHICH BRICK IS LAID

American - Horizontal rows of stretchers alternated by a row of headers

Common (or Stretcher) - Horizontal rows of bricks laid lengthwise

English - Alternating horizontal rows of stretchers and headers

Flemish - Alternating stretchers and headers within a horizontal row

Garden Wall - Alternating rows of Flemish and American bonds

Header - Horizontal rows of bricks laid endwise.

Roman - Horizontal rows of long, narrow pressed bricks laid lengthwise

STONE - MATERIAL COMPOSED OF MINERALS AND ANIMAL OR PLANT ELEMENTS; IN BUILD-INGS, MOST COMMON ARE LIMESTONE AND SANDSTONE

Limestone - Rock formed by the accumulation of rocks and shells and yielding lime when burned

Sandstone - Rock consisting of quartz and a cement such as silica or calcium carbonate formed by the action of wind and water

STONE COURSING - PATTERN IN WHICH STONE IS LAID

Broken Course Cut Stone - Randomly placed stones which have been cut into rectangles of various sizes

Cobblestone - Randomly placed stones of a size larger than a pebble and smaller than a boulder

Coursed Cut Stone - Rhythmically placed stone which has been cut into rectangles of uniform size

Coursed Rubble - Rhythmically placed stone as it comes from the quarry

Field Panel - Vertically placed stone of uniform size

Fieldstone - Randomly placed rocks found in fields, forest, etc.

Random Rubble - Unpatterned placing of rough quarry stone

Squared Rubble - Rhythmically placed quarry stone which has squared edges

STONE FINISH - SURFACE CHARACTERISTICS AND APPEARANCE OF STONE

Natural - Unchanged from original condition

<u>Polished</u> - Resulting in a smooth, glossy surface

<u>Rock-Faced</u> - Smooth band surrounding and recessed from natural section

<u>Rusticated</u> - Smooth band surrounding and recessed from smooth interior section

<u>Sown</u> - Series of carved lines creating a pattern

<u>Smooth Dressed</u> - Non-textured, flat surface

<u>Tooled (or Hammered)</u> - Random finish made with hand tools

<u>Vermiculated</u> - Smooth band surrounding and recessed from an interior plane having wavy lines

CONCRETE - MATERIAL CONSISTING OF CEMENT, SAND OR GRAVEL, AND WATER ALLOWED TO SET AND HARDEN

<u>Block</u> - Rhythmically placed, uniformly sized rectangles

<u>Plain, Pre-Cast Panel</u> - Flat, molded concrete pieces of uniform size

<u>Poured</u> - Liquid concrete poured into a frame and allowed to set and harden

<u>Shaped, Pre-Cast Panel</u> - Functionally or decoratively molded concrete pieces of uniform size

STUCCO - PORTLAND CEMENT, SAND AND LIME COMBINED, APPLIED IN A SOFT STATE, AND ALLOWED TO HARDEN; APPLIED OVER MASONRY

BOARD - SIDING UTILIZING THIN SAWED LUMBER WITH

LENGTH GREATLY EXCEEDING WIDTH

<u>Ashlar Imitation</u> - Wood cut and placed to resemble laid stone

<u>Board and Batten</u> - Vertical wood siding consisting of flat boards with narrow projecting strips covering the joints

<u>Clapboard</u> - Narrow, overlapping horizontal boards

<u>Flush Board</u> - Horizontal siding grooved together with an overlap

<u>Plank</u> - Vertically or horizontally laid siding with no overlap

<u>Shingle</u> - Wedge shaped piece of wood used in overlapping courses

<u>Shiplap</u> - Beveled jointed board siding laid horizontally

<u>Weatherboard</u> - Overlapping, horizontally laid wood siding

METAL - MATERIAL WHICH CAN BE MELTED, SHAPED, AND HARDENED INTO VARIOUS FORMS

<u>Aluminum Siding</u> - Horizontally placed, overlapping metal siding

<u>Cast Iron</u> - Result of pouring melted iron into a mold and letting it set

<u>Galvanized</u> - Result of coating iron or steel in molten zinc

<u>Metal and Glass</u> - Combination of molten forms of metal and glass used in sections

<u>Metal Sheet</u> - Metal which can be applied in sheets as siding

ROOFS

Complex - Combination of more than one roof style

Dome - Hemispherical in form

Flat - Having no pitch; horizontal

Gable - Having two slopes divided by a ridge and resulting in triangular end wall forms

Gambrel - Gable having two slopes on either side of a ridge, the lower slopes being the steeper ones

Hip - Having slopes on all four sides as well as a ridge line

Jerkinhead - Gable roof whose triangular ends feature a slope

Mansard - A truncated hip roof with a large flat surface and steep slopes

Pyramid - Having slopes on all four sides and coming to a point at the top

Saltbox - Gable roof whose slopes are unequal, providing two stories at front and one story at rear

Shed - Having one sloped plane

Truncated Hip - Hip whose slopes are interrupted by a flat section at the top

ROOFING MATERIALS

Asbestos - A fibrous, fire-resistant material derived from minerals

Asphalt - Made from the residue of petroleum refining

Cedar Shingles - Machine cut overlapping layers of cedar

Slate - Overlapping shingles composed of pressed, sealed rock

Standing Seam Sheet Metal - Attached panels anchored to a beam system, usually of copper or tin

CHIMNEYS

CHIMNEY - A FLUE FOR CONDUCTING SMOKE AND GASES FROM ABOVE A FIRE TO THE OUTSIDE AIR, USUALLY OF BRICK OR STONE

CHIMNEY POT - A SHORT EXTENSION OF A FLUE, USUALLY OF EARTHENWARE, TO INCREASE THE DRAFT

STOVEPIPE - SHEET METAL PIPE USED AS A STOVE CHIMNEY

WINDOWS AND DOORS

FRAME - A WOOD OR METAL ENCLOSING, SUPPORTING CASE INTO WHICH A WINDOW OR DOOR FITS

Elliptical - An arch whose head is broader than semi-circular

Flat - Having no arch; horizontal

Lancet - A sharply pointed arch

Ogee - A pointed arch composed of reverse curves

Segmental - An arch with a less than semi-circular curve

Semi-Circular - An arch with a round head

JAMB - VERTICAL FRAME OR SUPPORT

MULLION - A NARROW VERTICAL
SEPARATION USED FOR
DECORATION OR SUPPORT

PANE - A FRAMED SHEET OF
GLASS

SILL - HORIZONTAL PIECE AT
THE BOTTOM OF DOOR OR
WINDOW

Lugsill- Sill which does project beyond
the jamb

Slipsill - Sill which does not project
beyond the jamb

WINDOW CONFIGURATION -
RELATIVE ARRANGEMENT OR
PATTERN, USUALLY CON-
TROLLED BY THE SHAPE OF
THE FRAME

Bull's Eye - Round window

Diamond - Having four sides of equal
length, hung on the diagonal

Eyebrow - Semi-circular with horizontal
sill; half-round

Fanlight - Semi-circular or semi-
elliptical window with radial
mullions set over another window or
a door; presenting the appearance of
an opened fan

Oval - Egg-shaped

Quarter-Round - Pie shaped with a right
angle

Rectangular - Having four sides with
parallel sides having equal length
and meeting at right angles

Sidelight - A window flanking a door or
another window

Square - Having four sides of equal
length meeting at right angles

Transom - Opening over a door or
window, for decoration or ventilation

NOTE: *Windows may be made to fit the
shape of frames defined previously*

WINDOW OPERATION - METHOD
OF OPENING AND CLOSING

Casement - Swinging inward or outward
on pairs of hinges attached to the
jambs

Fixed - Non-operable, immovable

Hinged - Swinging inward or outward
on hinges attached to the jamb

Sash - Vertically movable; can be
single, double, or triple hung

Sliding - Horizontally movable; can be
single or multiple tracks

BAY WNDOW - WINDOW IN A
WALL PROJECTING FROM
ANOTHER WALL

Oriel - Bay window supported by
brackets

Polygonal - Multi-sided, non-right
angular bay

Rectangular - Three-sided, right angular
bay

DORMER WINDOW - VERTICALLY
SET WINDOW PROTRUDING
THROUGH A SLOPED ROOF

Eyelid - Low curved roof dormer with
reverse end curves giving it the
general outline of an eyelid

Porthole - Round roof dormer

Roof Dormer - Dormer emerging completely from a roof

Wall Dormer - Dormer created by the upward extension of a wall and breaking the roof line

DOOR PANEL - A THIN PIECE OF WOOD SET IN A FRAME

WINDOW AND DOOR TRIM

SURROUND - FRAMING AROUND WINDOW OR DOOR OPENING, DECORATIVE OR FUNCTIONAL

Hood Mould - Molding around top and sides of opening to deflect rain; also called label

Keystone - Wedge-shaped center of a hood mould or arch

Lintel - Horizontal structural member that extends across the top of the opening

Pediment - Triangular shaped decorative piece

Pilaster - Attached pier split lengthwise, frequently in same style as accompanying columns or piers

Soldier Arch - Brick lined on end with edge to front as structural support

SHUTTERS - EXTRA CLOSING OVER A DOOR OR WINDOW TO PREVENT ADMISSION OF LIGHT, RAIN, SNOW, ETC., USUALLY HUNG ON HINGES FROM JAMBS; CAN USUALLY BE LOUVERED OR SOLID

AWNINGS - SHELTERING SCREEN OVER A WINDOW, DOOR, WALKWAY, ETC.

TOWERS, TURRETS, AND CUPOLAS

CUPOLA - A DECORATIVE STRUCTURE EMERGING FROM THE MAIN ROOF STRUCTURE, FREQUENTLY OF A SIZE TO PROVIDE SITTING SPACE FOR ONE OR MORE PERSONS

TOWER - TALL STRUCTURE RISING TO A GREATER HEIGHT THAN ITS SURROUNDINGS

Battlement - A parapet built with indentations, for defense or decorative; crenellation

Parapet - Low retaining wall at the edge of a roof, porch, or terrace

TURRET - A SMALL TOWER, USUALLY EMERGING FROM A CORNER OF A BUILDING

ENTRIES, PORCHES, AND BALCONIES

BALCONY - PROJECTING RAILED PLATFORM IN FRONT OF A WINDOW OR DOOR

CANOPY - COVERED AREA EXTENDING FROM A BUILDING WALL TO PROTECT AN ENTRY

ENTRY - PLACE USED TO ENTER, USUALLY IDENTIFIED BY THE PRESENCE OF A DOOR

Soffit - Finished underside of an opening

PORCH - ROOFED AND FLOORED
SPACE OUTSIDE MAIN WALLS
OF A BUILDING, INCLUDES
SPACE FOR AN ENTRANCE

PORTICO - ENTRANCE PORCH

PORTE COCHERE - COACH OR
CARRIAGE PORCH; SHELTER
FOR VEHICLES OUTSIDE AN
ENTRY

VERANDAH - PORCH EXTENDING
THE LENGTH OF A BUILDING

Ancone - Scrolled bracket or console,
support for an entry cornice

Baluster - An upright support for a rail

Balustrade - A series of balusters joined
by a rail, serving as an enclosure for
balconies, staircases, etc.

Capital - Head of a column

Column - Free standing, vertical support
pillar

Latticework - Diagonal or crossed
network of wood or metal used as an
airy, ornamental screening

Pier - Vertical masonry support

Post - Vertical wood or metal support

OUTBUILDINGS

GARAGE - STORAGE SHELTER
FOR AUTOMOBILES IN CON-
JUNCTION WITH A RESIDENCE

GAZEBO - AN OPEN SHELTER
BUILT FOR A VIEW

STORAGE SHEDS - ENCLOSED
SHELTER USED FOR STORAGE

ORNAMENTATION

DETAILING - AN ELEMENT OF
DESIGN TO WHICH PARTICU-
LAR ATTENTION IS PAID;
FUNCTIONAL OR DECORATIVE

Beltcourse - A flat, horizontal band
marking story divisions

Bracket - A projection from the face of a
wall under eaves, window, or porch

Diamond Shingles - Wooden or slate
shingles arranged in rows and shaped
like diamonds; diagonally laid
shingles

Fishscales - Wooden or slate shingles in
a fishscale shape arranged in rows

GINGERBREAD - DETAILING
SERVING NO FUNCTIONAL
PURPOSE

Bargeboard - Vertical board set into the
roof edge of a gable; vergeboard

Cresting - Decorative ridge for a roof; a
series of finials; balustrade at a
widow's walk

Finial - An ornament at the top of a
spire, gable, or finial

Pendant - An ornament suspended from
above

Scrollwork - Open cut work with a
jigsaw

Sunburst - Carving frequently set in a
pediment consisting of a hemisphere
with radials.

Swag - Simulated net-held mass of fruit
and flowers sagging between two
supports

Tracery - Curving openwork shapes
creating a pattern

FENCES

FENCE - A FREE STANDING, SELF-SUPPORTING STRUCTURE OF METAL, MASONRY, COMPOSITION, OR WOOD OR ANY COMBINATION THEREOF RESTING ON OR PARTIALLY BURIED IN THE GROUND AND RISING ABOVE GROUND LEVEL, AND USED FOR CONFINEMENT, SCREENING, OR PARTITION PURPOSES

Board - Vertically placed narrow pieces of wood laid side-by-side

Brick - Usually used in combination with other fence as supports

Picket - Combination of vertically placed pointed stakes

Stockade - Sections of joined vertical boards

Wrought Iron - Commercial form of iron that is tought, yet bendable

LANDSCAPING

LANDSCAPING - IMPROVEMENT OF A LOT, PARCEL, OR TRACT OF LAND WITH GRASS AND SHRUBS AND/OR TREES. LANDSCAPING IS DESIGNED AND ARRANGED TO PRODUCE AN AESTHETICALLY PLEASING EFFECT

Ground Cover - Low plantings which spread over an area of land

Grass - Vertical growing narrow leafed plants of a low height

Shrubs - Low growing woody plants

Trees - Tall growing woody plants, usually with one elongated stem

SIGNS

SIGN - NAME, IDENTIFICATION, DESCRIPTION, DISPLAY, OR ILLUSTRATION WHICH IS AFFIXED TO OR PAINTED UPON OR REPRESENTED DIRECTLY OR INDIRECTLY UPON A BUILDING, STRUCTURE, OR PIECE OF LAND OR AFFIXED TO THE GLASS ON THE OUTSIDE OR INSIDE OF A WINDOW SO AS TO BE SEEN FROM THE OUTSIDE OF A BUILDING AND WHICH DIRECTS ATTENTION TO AN OBJECT, PRODUCT, PLACE, PERSON, INSTITUTION, ORGANIZATION, OR BUSINESS

Billboard - Large, free-standing panel designed to carry outdoor advertising; also known as poster panels

Flashing - Illluminated sign which exhibits change in color or intensity

Free Standing - Suspended by one or more braces in the ground surface; braces are 30 inches or more in length

Ground Projecting - Suspended by one or more braces in the ground surfaces; braces are 30 inches in length

Illuminating - Artificially lighted

Moving - Rotating or otherwise in motion

Portable - Sign attached to a structure not permanently affixed to the ground or wall

Suspended - Supported by braces attached to the building to which the sign relates

MESSAGE - THEME BEING COMMUNICATED

Advertising - Sign directing attention to a use, service, or commodity not related to the premises

Identification - Displaying name, address, product, service, and/or other data pertinent to the use of the premises

PATIOS AND DECKS

DECK - AN OPEN OUTDOOR AREA ADJOINING A HOUSE, CONSTRUCTED OF WOOD, THE HEIGHT OF WHICH IS LESS THAN 8 INCHES ABOVE THE AVERAGE LEVEL OF THE ADJOINING GROUND

PATIO - AN OPEN OUTDOOR AREA ADJOINING A HOUSE, CONSTRUCTED OF MASONRY, THE HEIGHT OF WHICH IS LESS THAN 8 INCHES ABOVE THE AVERAGE LEVEL OF THE ADJOINING GROUND

STEPS AND WALKS

SIDEWALK - A WALK AT THE SIDE OF A STREET

STEPS - OUTDOOR STAIRS PROVIDING ACCESS BETWEEN A WALK AND A PORCH OR ENTRY

WALK - AN ARRANGED OR PAVED PATH FOR WALKING

WIDOW'S WALK - A RAILED OBSERVATION PLATFORM ATOP A HOUSE

BIBLIOGRAPHY

BOOKS

American Victorian Architecture: A Survey of the 70's and 80's in Contemporary Photographs. New York: Dover Pulbications, Inc., 1975.

Blumenson, John J.G. Identifying American Architecture. Nashville: American Association for State and Local History, 1977.

Brooks, H. Allen. The Prairie School. New York: W.W. Norton, 1972.

City of Oakland Planning Department. Rehab Right Oakland, 1978.

The Downtown Development Office. Richmond Architectural Renovation. Richmond, Virginia.

Evert, L. H. Combination Atlas Map of Montgomery County, Ohio. 1875.

Favretti, Rudy J. and Joy Putnam Favretti. Landscapes and Gardens for Historic Buildings. Nashville: American Association for State and Local History, 1978.

Foley, Mary Mix. The American House. New York: Haprer and Row, 1980.

Harris, Cyril M. Historic Architecture Sourcebook. New York: McGraw - Hill, 1977.

Karp, Ben. Ornamental Carpentry on Nineteenth Century American Houses. New York: Dover Publications, 1981.

Legner, Linda, compiler. City House: A Guide to Renovating Older Chicago-Area Houses. Chicago: Chicago Review Press, Inc., 1979.

Leighton, Ann. American Gardens of the Nineteenth Century. Amherst: University of Massachusetts Press, 1987.

McAlester, Virginia and Lee. A Field Guide to American Houses. New York: Alfred A. Knopf, 1986.

Maass, John. The Gingerbread Age: A View of Victorian America. New York: Greenwich House, 1983.

Moss, Roger. Century of Color: Exterior Decoration for American Buildings, 1820-1920. Watkins Glen, New York: American Life Foundation, 1981.

National Decorative Products Association, Inc. Paint Problem Solver. St. Louis, Missouri, 1980.

National Trust for Historic Preservation. Old and New Architecture: Design Relationship. Washington, D.C.: Preservation Press, 1980.

Rifkind, Carole. A Field Guide to American Architecture. New York: The New American Library, 1980.

Whiffen, Marcus. American Architecture Since 1780: A Guide to the Styles. Cambridge, Massachusetts: MIT Press, 1981.

PERIODICALS

Clark, Susan. "Make Your Own Ornamental Wood Screens." The Old-House Journal. Vol. IX, No. 7, July 1981.

Diedrich, James, G., American Building Restoration, Inc. "Specify the Correct...Masonry Sealers." The Old-House Journal. Vol. III, No. 2, November 1975.

Flaherty, Carolyn. "Sawn Wood Ornamentation." The Old-House Journal. Vol. II, No. 7. July 1974.

"Flat Roof Repairs." The Old-House Journal. Vol. I, No. 1 October 1973.

Gelbloom, Mara. "Old Storefronts, 1870-1920." The Old-House Journal. Vol. VI, No. 7, March 1978.

Gerhardt, Tom. "Victorian Cast Iron Fountains and Urns." The Old-House Journal. Vol. V, Nos. 6 and 7, June and July 1977.

Goode, Stacy Jackson. "Building an Old Fashioned Garden." The Old-House Journal. Vol. VI, No. 2, February 1978.

Herman, Frederick, AIA. "Fences, Parts I, II, III." The Old-House Journal. Vol. VII, Nos. 2, 3, and 4, February, March, and April 1979.

_____. "Masonry Re-pointing." The Old-House Journal. Vol. VII, No. 6 , June 1979.

_____. "Restoring Old Brickwork." The Old-House Journal. Vol. III, No. 3, March 1975.

Horton, Eva, Kristia Associates. "Chimney Sweeping." The Old-House Journal. Vol. V, No. 5, May 1977.

Jeanloz, Donna. "Victorian Landscaping." The Old-House Journal. Vol. V, No. 4, April 1977.

Kitchen, Judith. "Masonry Preservation Guided by Material Properties." Echoes. August 1975.

Labine, Ronald A. Clem. "Defeating Decay." The Old-House Journal. Vol. IX, No. 5, May 1981.

_____. "Don't Blame the Paint." The Old-House Journal. Vol. IX, No. 4, April 1981.

_____. "Repairing Slate Roofs." The Old-House Journal. Vol. III, No. 12, December 1975.

_____. "Roofing: Repair or Replacement." The Old-House Journal. Vol. IX, No. 2, February 1981.

_____. "Tips on Stripping Shutters." The Old-House Journal. Vol. II, No. 9, September 1974.

Labine, Ronald A., Sr. and Ronald A. Labine, Jr. "Stripping Exterior Paint." The Old-House Journal. Vol. IX, No. 4, April 1981.

McConkey, James. "Fixing Double Hung Windows." The Old-House Journal. Vol. VII, No. 12, December 1979.

Meyer, C. R. "Roofing With Wood Shingles." The Old-House Journal. Vol. V, No. 8, August 1977.

Minnery, Catherine and Donald. "Repairing Stucco." The Old-House Journal. Vol. VII, No. 7, July 1979.

Mosca, Matthew J. "Historic Paint Research: Determining the Original

Colors." The Old-House Journal. Vol. IX, No. 4, April 1981.

Ohlerking, Robert. "Cast Iron." The Old-House Journal. Vol. VIII, No. 2, February 1980.

Perron, Robert. "Picket Fences." The Family Handyman. April 1982.

Pilling, Ron. "Brick Walks." The Old-House Journal. Vol. VIII, No. 7, July 1980.

Poore, Patricia. "It's Not As Easy As It Looks." The Old-House Journal. Vol. IX, No. 4, April 1981.

Prudon, Theodore. "The Case Against Removing the Paint From Brick Masonry." The Old-House Journal. Vol. III, No. 2, February 1975.

_____. "Removing Stains From Masonry." The Old-House Journal. Vol. V, No. 5, May 1977.

"Restoring Rotted Wood Sills." The Old-House Journal. Vol. II, No. 8, August 1974.

"Restoring Shutters to Working Order." The Old-House Journal. Vol. I, No. 2, November 1973.

"Screen Door Patterns." The Old-House Journal. Vol. VIII, No. 7, July 1980.

Special Window Issue. The Old-House Journal. Vol. X, No. 4, April 1982.

Technical Staff, The Old-House Journal. "Maintenance of Gutters." The Old-House Journal. Vol. VII, Nos. 10 and 11, October and November 1979.

_____. Part II: Major Repairs and Replacement Castings; Cast Iron." The Old-House Journal. Vol. VIII, No. 3, March 1980.

Wilson, H. Weber. "Window Glass." The Old-House Journal. Vol. VI, No. 4, April 1978.

Zirkle, John F. "Removing Exterior Paint." The Old-House Journal. Vol. VII, No. 6, June 1979.

LEAFLETS

Hartford Architecture Conservancy. "Landscaping the Old House." Spring 1979.

_____. "Saving Energy in the Old House." Winter 1980.

"How To Select and Use Latex Caulks." Rohm and Haas, Philadelphia, 1975.

Mack, Robert C. "The Cleaning and Waterproof Coating of Masonry Buildings." Preservation Briefs 1. Washington, D. C., 1975.

_____. "Repointing Mortar Joints in Historic Brick Buildings." Preservation Briefs 2. Washington, D. C., 1975.

National Paint and Coating Association, Inc. "Mildew." Technical Division Scientific Circular #802. Washington, D. C.

"Practical Paint Pointers." X.I.M. Products, Inc. 1972.

Sweetser, Sarah M. "Roofing For Historic Buildings." Preservation Briefs 4. Washington, D. C., 1978.

Sincere appreciation is extended to The
Old-House Journal, Inc. for its
wealth of rehabilitation expertise.
Additional information can be
obtained by writing to the company
at 69A Seventh Avenue, Brooklyn,
New York 11217.

Reprinting of any portion of Blueprint
for Rehabilitation is permitted only
after obtaining written authorization
from the City of Dayton, Department
of Planning, City Hall, 101 West
Third Street, Dayton, Ohio 45401.

The following Department of Planning
staff were responsible for the revised
and updated edition of this publication: Teresa Prosser and Tim D. Keefe.

May 1990

THE SECRETARY OF THE INTERIOR'S STANDARDS FOR REHABILITATION

1. Every resonable effort shall be made to provide a compatible use for a property which requires minimal alteration of the building structure or site and its environment, or to use a property for its originally intended purpose.

2. The distinguishing original qualities or character of a building, structure, or site and its environment shall not be destroyed. The removal or alteration of any historic material or distrinctive architectural features should be avoided when possible.

3. All buildings, structures, and sites shall be recognized as products of their own time. Alterations that have no historical basis and which seek to create an earlier appearance shall be discouraged.

4. Changes which may have taken place in the course of time are evidence of the history and development of a building, structure, or site and its environment. These changes may have acquired significance in their own right, and this significance shall be recognized and respected.

5. Distinctive stylistic features or examples of skilled craftsmanship which characterize a building, structure, or site shall be treated with sensitivity.

6. Deteriorated architectural features shall be repaired, rather than replaced, wherever possible. In the event replacement is necessary, the new material should match the material being replaced in composition, design, color, texture, and other visual qualities. Repair or replacement of missing architectural features should be based on accurate duplication of features, substantiated by historic plysical or pictorial evidence rather than on conjectural designs or the availability of different architectural ements from other buildings.

7. The surface cleaning of structures shall be undertaken with the gentlest means possible. Sandblasting and other cleaning methods that will damage the historic building materials shall not be undertaken.

8. Every reasonable effort shall be made to protect and preseve archaeo-logical resources affected by or adjacent to any project.

9. Contemporary design for alterations and additions to existing properties shall not be discouraged when such altera-tions and additions do not destroy significant historical, architectural, or cultural material, and such design is compatible with the size, scale, color, material and character of the property, neighborhoods, or environment.

10. Wherever possible, new additions or alterations to structures shall be done in such a manner that if such additions or alterations were to be removed in the future, the essential form and integrity of the structure would be unimpaired.